W9-CDC-479

A Garland Series

The English Stage
Attack and Defense 1577 - 1730

A collection of 90 important works
reprinted in photo-facsimile in 50 volumes

edited by
Arthur Freeman
Boston University

Mr. Law's Unlawfulness
of the Stage Entertainment Examin'd

The Entertainment of the Stage

Some Few Hints,
in Defence of Dramatical Entertainments

Allan Ramsay

with a preface
for the Garland Edition by

Arthur Freeman

Garland Publishing, Inc., New York & London

1974

Library of Congress Cataloging in Publication Data

Philomusus, S
    Mr. Law's Unlawfulness of the stage entertainment
examin'd.

    "The Entertainment of the stage" attributed to
George Anderson. Cf. pref.
    Reprint of the 3 works: the 1st, printed and sold
by J. Roberts, London, 1726; the 2d, printed by J.
Davidson, Edinburgh, 1727; and the 3d, published in 1728?
    1. Theater—Moral and religious aspects. 2. Law,
William, 1686-1761. The absolute unlawfulness of the
stage-entertainment fully demonstrated. I. The
Entertainment of the stage. 1974. II. Anderson,
George, 1676-1756. III. Ramsay, Allan, 1685-1758.
Some few hints, in defence of dramatical entertainments.
1974. IV. Title.
PN2047.P53   1974   792'.013   76-170496
ISBN 0-8240-0633-X

Preface

*Three more contributions to the Law "unlawful-
ness" controversy are contained in this volume. "S.
Philomusus" has not been identified; his antagon-
istic examination of Law is reprinted from a copy
in the Boston Public Library (G.3823.21), collating
A-D⁴ (Lowe-Arnott-Robinson 372). A reply to this
is by the preeminent Scottish poet, Allan Ramsay,
whose* Some Few Hints *(a very rare book) is dated
[1728] by Lowe-Arnott-Robinson (374), and,
probably correctly, [1727] by* NCBEL: for The
Entertainment of the Stage, *which is the response
in turn to Ramsay by George Anderson, Minister
of Tron Church, Edinburgh, bears an imprint of
1727 (Lowe-Arnott-Robinson 373). We reprint Ramsay's book from a copy in the University of Texas at
Austin (Ak.R147.728s), collating A-C⁴ (drop-title
only), and Anderson's (strictly anonymous) from a
copy in the British Museum (1343.a.3[2]), collating A-E⁴F². Both are of course Scottish, and
hence weltered by principle in the quarrel between
Northern orthodox theology and "apostatic" free-
thinking, some geographical and aesthetic remove
from the drama itself.*

May, 1973   A. F.

5

Mr. *L A W*'s

UNLAWFULNESS

OF THE

STAGE *Entertainment*

EXAMIN'D:

AND

The Insufficiency of his Arguments fully demonstrated.

By *S. PHILOMUSUS*, M.A.

LONDON,

Printed: And Sold by J. ROBERTS, in *Warwick-Lane.* 1726.

[*Price 6 Pence.*]

Mr. LAW's

Unlawfulness of the STAGE ENTERTAINMENT examin'd.

I Am fenfible how little Encouragement there is at prefent for writing Pamphlets, by the Small-nefs of the Number of Good Ones that appears among us. Accordingly, this was undertaken without the leaft mercenary View; and, if it falls into no other than the Hands of fuch whofe Judgments have been perverted by the Treatife it is in-tended to confute, I fhall be fatisfied. The Profpect of contributing, in ever fo flender a Degree, to the Happinefs and Welfare of Mankind, is what I am excited by, upon thefe Occafions.

But I will premife no further, becaufe I am going to cenfure our Author upon that Account who begins with a fort of an Introduction, letting us know how *fenfible he is that the Title of his Book will, to the Generality of People, feem too high a Flight; be look'd upon as the Effect of a fanatical Spirit, and carrying Matters higher than the Sobriety of Religion requires:* Upon which, he begs that *fuch* would *fufpend their Judgment for a while, and be content to read his Trea-tife, before they pafs any Judgment either upon the Me-rits of the Subject or the Temper of the Writer.*

Now I am of Opinion that it is not of any Con-cern to the World, what the Temper of this or any

other

other Writer is; but, if the Tendency of their Writings is like to be prejudicial to Mankind, it is proper they should be taken in hand and examin'd, and the Falsity and Insufficiency of them expos'd and detected. This must be my Apology for meddling with Mr. L a w's Book. For tho' there is nothing of any real Weight or Force in it, yet there is enough to distract and perplex the Minds of those who are not us'd to Arguments, to rob them of the Peace and Tranquility of Innocence, and terrify their Souls with the shocking Appearance of imaginary Guilt. Neither would the pernicious Mischief end here; but such Notions as his, if they were to prevail, would be apt to spoil the Growth and discourage the Use of Dramatic Performances; which, in all Ages and Countries in the World, have always been esteem'd the most noble and improving Diversions, that the Mind, at its Hours of Leisure and Recreation, could be entertain'd with. I shall make this appear occasionally as I go along; intending to examine his Arguments and Demonstrations, as he calls them, in order as they ly before me.

P. 1. He begins with making a Comparison between *worshipping Images*, and *going to Plays*, and thinks that they who own the Unlawfulness of the one, ought to be convinc'd of the Sinfulness of the other. This is his first Argument, and takes up the Five first Pages of his Book. The Insufficiency of which the Reader may easily perceive from the following Particulars. 1. *Worshipping Images* is certainly a great and notorious Sin, being not only contrary to an express Command of God, but to common Sense and Reason; and therefore, in some measure, criminal even in mere Heathens. But *going to Plays*, in general, is no where forbidden in Scripture, nor in any respect contrary to Sense and Reason, but rather

agree-

agreeable to both. 2. The Author in this Place, and indeed throughout his whole Book, begs the Question which he ought to prove, *that it is sinful to go to a Play.* Whenever that can be made appear, I will joyn my Endeavours in dissuading the World from it, as heartily and sincerely as he can do. 3. That there are in some Plays, things which must certainly give Offence to People of a chast Ear, and refin'd way of Thinking, I cannot deny. But then these are accidental Evils, depending sometimes upon a vicious Poet; sometimes upon an impudent Player, over-acting his Part; and often upon the bad Taste of an Audience, who, generally speaking, have it in their Power to model the Manners of the Stage just as they please, by shewing their Approbation or Dislike upon proper Occasions. But this makes no more against the Lawfulness and Propriety of Stage-Entertainments in general, than a buffoon, ridiculous Preacher would against going to Church. The End of Dramatic Entertainments is, by giving a Picture of some Parts of human Life, to recommend to the Audience the Practice of Honour, Politeness, and in a word, every moral Virtue; and to discourage the Imitation of any thing Scandalous and Disagreeable, by shewing it in its own odious and ridiculous Light. Now if this End is defeated by any of those accidental Abuses I mention'd before, the Guilt of such Indecencies is not to be imputed to any but those who actually commit them, or designedly incourage them: no more than they who go to Church, with an honest Intention of paying their Devotions, are chargeable with the Impertinence, Enthusiasm, Rant and Nonsense, with which they are sometimes entertain'd from the Pulpit. There is no arguing therefore against the Use of a thing in general, from the Abuses of it commited by Particulars: As this Author does,

who

who makes no Exceptions; but affirms throughout his whole Book, without the least Shadow of a Proof, that *going to Plays*, in general, is as unlawful and sinful, as *Idolatry*, Drunkenness, Murder, Theft, Adultery, and what not; Things, which tho' they had never been forbidden by an express Law from Heaven, are so manifestly and unexceptionably *mala in se*; always unreasonable, always wicked.

To give the Reader a Specimen of his Reasoning, says he (pag. 4.) *You go to hear a Play: I tell you that you go to hear Ribaldry and Profaneness; that you entertain your Mind with extravagant Thoughts, wild Rant, blasphemous Speeches, wanton Amours, profane Jests, and impure Passions. If you ask me, where is the Sin of all this? You may as well ask me where is the Sin of Swearing and Lying. For it is not only a Sin against this or that particular Text of Scripture, but it is a Sin against the whole Nature and Spirit of our Religion.* I have transcrib'd this whole Paragraph at once, to give the Reader a View of our Author's way of arguing and thinking upon this Subject. People say, *they go to hear a Play*; he says, *they lye:* he knows what they go to hear better than they do themselves. They go upon no other Account, but *to hear Ribaldry and Prophaneness, and to entertain their Minds with wanton Amours and impure Passions.* And, in doing thus, they are guilty of as great Sins as those of *Swearing and Lying,* &c.

From this and many other Places in his Treatise, it is manifest that this Author makes it equally as criminal to represent Vices upon the Stage, and be present at the representing them, as actually to perpetrate and commit them. Whereas, in representing the Manners of the Age, in order to expose the Vices and Follies of it, it is necessary the Players should personate Characters of all sorts, and the Audience employ their Minds in thinking and reflecting upon them; which both may do, if they please, as in-

nocently

nocently as *one* may write, and *others* read an Histo-ry, which gives an Account of the Commiſſion of the moſt unlawful and deteſtable Crimes. The Bible itſelf deſcribes Murders and Adulteries, with moſt other enormous Sins, in a ſtrong Light: Which I hope may be allow'd to be read, without ſuppoſing the Mind of the Reader to be inſpired with Senti-ments in favour of Cruelty or Luſt. According to his way of Arguing, if it is criminal to give a Theatrical Deſcription of *wanton Amours*, and *impure Paſſions*, by the ſame Rule the Actors have been guilty of Murder, Treaſon, &c. a thou-ſond times over; and the beſt Part of the King's Sub-jects have been aiding and aſſiſting to them therein. This ſingle Obſervation muſt needs convince the Reader, upon what a wrong miſtaken Foundation this Author has built his whole Invective againſt Stage Entertainments in general: For as to thoſe real Indecencies, which I deny not but are ſome-times to be found in our Theatres, I am far enough from making any Defence or Apology for them; I give them up; and wiſh with all my Heart the World would agree to be ſo ſenſible and well-bred as to explode them all.

And here I ſhall take leave of my Author's *firſt* Argument; deſiring the Reader to obſerve, that he has prov'd nothing all this while; but laid down an Aſſertion, which no one will ever diſpute with him, that, *When it is ſinful to go to a Play, it is ſinful:* for, as to its being generally and always ſo, tho' he has often affirm'd it, he has not made the leaſt Step towards proving and making it out. I grant that *Entertainments which awaken our diſorder'd Paſſions, and teach to reliſh Lewdneſs, immoral Rant, and Pro-phaneneſs, are exceeding ſinful,* and that People are to be blam'd for being preſent at them; provided it can be made appear, that ſuch Entertainments were

pre-

prepar'd with such an Intent by the Composers of them; and that accordingly they always and certainly have such an Effect upon the Audience. Otherwise all the Sermons that ever were preach'd against Fornication and Adultery, Riot and Intemperance of any sort, may be said to be *exceeding sinful*; because, they often describe the Nature and Extent of those Crimes; and, by this means, put the Audience in mind of them. But, as no one ever pretended, that Sermons, which treated of such Topics, were, for that Reason only, *exceeding sinful*; neither can the same be said of Plays, written and acted upon the same Account, and consequently producing the same Effects.

Yet how does he triumph, after having done nothing (p. 5.) with a *Thus stands the first Argument against the Stage: It has all the Weight in it, that the whole Weight of Religion can give to any Argument.* And then *(p. 6.)* with the same triumphal Air he proceeds to his

Secondly, Let the next Argument against the Stage be taken from its manifest Contrariety to this important Passage of Scripture; Let no Communication proceed out of your Mouth, but that which is good to the Use of edifying; that it may minister Grace to the Hearers: and grieve not the holy Spirit of God, whereby ye are seal'd to the Day of Redemption. Here again, with this pompous Argument, he does nothing but what he did before, beg the Question; by taking it for granted, that all theatrical Entertainments are intended and designed to promote Vice and Immorality. Whereas in all wise and well-ordered Governments, and, I sincerely believe, in our own, they are allowed for a quite contrary End, *viz.* to expose Vice and ill Behaviour of all sorts to the Ridicule and Contempt, and to recommend an honest agreeable Deportment to the Imitation, of the Audience. He

should

should prove, that all Plays were intended with such bad Designs, and generally produce such bad Effects, before he can argue against them as *corrupt Communication*, and as something which is not *good to the use of edifying*. This he ought to prove in the first place. But, instead of that, he goes a short way to work, and takes it for granted; and then, very demurely, asks this Question: *If it be unlawful to have any corrupt Communication of our own, can we think it lawful to go to Places set apart for that Purpose?* He seems here to have been let into a very great political Secret; which, if true, those concern'd ought not to thank him for the Discovery of, *viz.* that our Theatres, which are authoriz'd by the Permission, and have been frequently honour'd by the Presence of our Sovereigns, as well as the best of their Subjects, are *set apart for no other Purpose but corrupt and unedifying Communication*; and for People to be entertained with *Oaths and Imprecations, Prophaneness and Impurity of Discourse.*

—— *Quorsum hæc tam putida tendunt?*

If the Author's Allegations were true, I am ready to grant that neither the Quality nor Character of any Person ought to be us'd as a Skreen to an unlawful Action; but, in the mean time, I shall take the Liberty to charge him with having laid down a very false and seditious Position: in affirming, that the Play-house is *a House set apart for corrupt Communications.*

It is with the same presuming Air, that he goes on (*p. 7.*) taking it for granted, that Women (who go to Play-houses) *frequent such Places to hear Oaths*, and give their Money to see Women *forget the Modesty of their Sex, and talk impudently in a public Play-house.* He should not wonder to see *Rakes and ill Women* do thus. But for Persons, *who profess Purity and Holiness*, &c. for *them to give their Money to be thus entertained, is such a Contradiction to all Piety and common*

B *Sense*

Sense, as cannot be sufficiently expos'd. When he is able to prove that the Ladies, who frequent our Theatres, do generally *give their Money* with a Defign only *to hear Oaths, and fee Women forget the Modefty of their Sex,* &c. I fhall be very ready to grant that this will be *fuch a Contradiction to all Piety and common Senfe as cannot be sufficiently expos'd.* But if they go with a Defign to be improv'd, by feeing Virtue, Difcretion and Good-breeding agreeably recommended, and Vice and Folly expos'd; I fhall think they are no more to anfwer for fome few Indecencies which may happen to be mixed with fuch Reprefentations, than they, who go to Church to ferve God, and to be improv'd by the religious Difcourfe of a grave Divine, are chargeable with contributing to the treafonable Infinuations, grofs Defcriptions of irregular Paffions, Nonfenfe and Abfurdities, which are fometimes uttered from the Pulpit.

Such hitherto is the poor way of arguing our Author contents himfelf with; yet he concludes his *fecond* Argument with his ufual Triumph, by faying, (p. 7.) *If therefore I was to reft here, I might fairly fay, that I had prov'd the Stage to be as contrary to Scripture, as the Worfhip of Images is contrary to the fecond Commandment.* Whereas he has *prov'd* nothing; but ignorantly taken it for granted, that both Players and Spectators are actually guilty of thofe innumerable Vices and Follies which are fabuloufly reprefented upon the Stage: At which rate, as I obferved before, he may as well charge them with the Guilt of Murder, as any thing elfe.

Let us *now,* with our Author, (p. 8.) *proceed to a third Argument againft the Stage.* And here, according to his former profound way of reafoning, he takes it for granted that *Players were never fufpected to be Perfons of Chriftian Piety. That the Bu-*

finefs

*sine*ss of a Player is *prophane, wicked, lewd and immo-*
*de*ft; and *challenges any one to shew him that it is a more*
Christian Employment than that of Robbers. He affirms, that *it is abominably sinful, and inconsistent with*
the Christian Religion; and places it *amongst the most*
abominable Crimes, (*p. 9,* 10.) and from thence in-
fers (as with good Reason he might, if it were so)
that *they* cannot be *innocent who delight in their Sins,*
and hire them to commit them. This Argument (as he
says) *is not far-fetch'd, or founded on any Subtleties of*
Reasoning. No truly; if you eat your Pudding
while it is too hot, it will certainly burn you. But
to destroy this whole Argument at once, and to answer the *Challenge* he gives for any one *to shew him*
that the Business of Players is a more Christian Em-
ployment than that of Robbers; I shall only put him
in Mind, once more, that the Business of a Player
is, by thus much, a more Christian Employment than
that of a Robber; as it is less criminal in a Painter
to paint a Robbery, than actually to commit one;
in an Historian, to describe a barbarous and bloody
Murder, than actually to be concern'd in it; and in
a Clergyman, to represent to his Congregation the
odious Appearance and ill Consequences of Lewdness and Drunkenness, than actually to be guilty of
those Sins himself. Whether Players are modest or
immodest, sober or intemperate off of the Stage, is
nothing to our present Purpose; no more than it is
for a Lady of nice Virtue to be concern'd whether
her Coach-horses are Creatures of a chaste Disposition or not: provided they look well, and carry her
with Spirit from one Visit to another, she has no
Objection against them. I think Players, as to what
concerns their Employment, may be as good Christians as Poets, Painters, Historiographers, or Divines; and have as much Right, as any of these, to
represent *Lust, Prophaneness, and disordered Passions.*

B 2　　　　　　　My

My Knowledge of their private Lives and Conver-
fations is but little. But I can venture to affirm of
one of them, with whom I have fome Acquaintance,
that I don't know a more modeſt, pious, well-be-
hav'd Chriſtian. Every one who knows Mr. *Mills*
will fee by this Defcription that I mean him: Tho'
I have good Reaſon to believe the fame might be
faid of feveral others among them. But, be that as
it will, I can't fee the leaſt Reaſon, nor has our Author difcovered the leaſt, why, as Players, they
fhould be accounted *the moſt vile and abominable Sin-
ners.* Therefore till he proves that repreſenting and
defcribing Sins is as criminal as really committing
them, he ought to make a public Recantation of
this uncharitable Slander; and ask Forgiveneſs as
well of thefe injured People, as of the Audience, to
whom, by their Prefence and Participation, he im-
putes the fame Guilt.

His *fourth Argument* (p. 11.) ſtands thus: As the Church
is the Houſe of God, and, by what is there exhibited,
tends to the Promotion of Piety and Religion; fo the
Play-houſe is *the Devil's Houſe, where profligate Per-
fons of both Sexes are beating and inflaming one another
with all the Wantonneſs of Addreſs, the Immodeſty of
Motion, and Lewdneſs of Thought, that Wit can invent:*
It is therefore juſt as wrong to go to the one, as
it is right to go to the other. Here, it is to be obferved, that he again begs the Queſtion, by ſuppoſing the Play-houſe to be *the Devil's Houſe,* &c.
For, in reality, the Play-houſe, when it is not a-
bufed, differs no otherwife from the Houſe of God,
than that the one is a Place for true Devotion, the
other for innocent Diverſion and honeſt Recreation.
At one, we do, or ought to, improve our felves;
by hearing the Law of God read and explain'd to us;
at the other we do, or ought to do, the fame; by
feeing the Ways of the World repreſented in a very
lively

lively manner; that which is truly commendable, heighten'd and embellished with all the Charms that an ingenious Fancy can give it; and that which is really detestable, expos'd and ridicul'd with all the Art and Dexterity that an agreeable Wit can furnish. Thus Plays are, or ought to be: This is the End and Design of them, when they are not perverted and abus'd. However, that they may be, and are sometimes, debas'd to ill Purposes, is no more an Argument against the general Use of them, than it would be against going to Church, because Atheists, Pick-pockets and common Strumpets do sometimes go thither; and Sedition, Nonsense, and Enthusiasm are sometimes preach'd there. Honest, well-meaning People may certainly keep up their Integrity in both Places, and improve themselves proportionably in both; notwithstanding the bad Company they may chance to be mixt with: The Service of God and the Devil, depending, not upon this or that Place merely, but upon the Mind and Inclinations of those that frequent them. Some People serve God at a Play-house, better than others do at Church; and some serve the Devil more at Church, than others do at the Play-house. Pick-pockets and Strumpets are the same where-ever they happen to be.

Tectum non animum mutant. ——

He runs on (in p. 14. and 15.) upon this ridiculous Supposition, that the Play-house is *the Devil's House,* and rings the Changes upon his own *Postulatum* with great Pleasure. *If therefore (says he) we may say that a House or Festival was the Devil's, because he was delighted with it; because what was there done, was an acceptable Service to him; we may be assured that the Play-house is as really the House of the Devil, as any other House ever was. Nay, it is reasonable to think that the Play-houses in this Kingdom are a greater Pleasure to him than any*

Temple

Temple he ever had in the *Heathen World*. How he comes to be fo well acquainted with the Devil's Tafte I cannot imagine. But, if I may be allow'd to ghefs at it, I fhould think he was far better pleas'd with that ferious fincere Worfhip, accompanied with the moft immoral intemperate Rites, which was paid him by the Heathens, under the Titles of *Venus*, *Bacchus*, &c. than he can be by an Affembly of *Chriftians*, who heartily deteft him and all his Works; who are thoroughly convinc'd that the *Venus*, the *Bacchus*, &c. prefented to their View, are the Likeneffes of thofe falfe Gods which were worfhip'd by the Heathens of old; but which, at the fame time, are fo far from being rever'd and ador'd by thefe *Chriftians*, that they treat them with the utmoft Contempt; ufe them to the fame End they do Fools and Buffoons; to excite their Mirth, by the ridiculous Appearance of fuch a mock Reprefentation. For my part, I cannot devife any means how a Set of falfe Gods can be treated with greater Contempt than they are upon thefe Occafions. But (fays the Author) *what though Hymns and Adorations are not offer'd to impure and filthy Deities, yet if Impurity and Filthinefs is the Entertainment; if immodeft Songs, prophane Rant, if Luft and Paffion entertain the Audience, the Bufinefs is the fame, and the Affembly does the fame Honour to the Devil, though they be not gather'd together in the Name of fome Heathen God.*

Here lies the Strefs of this whole Argument; and the Weight of it depends upon thefe Particulars; *firft*, whether *Impurity and Filthinefs be the Entertainment*; *fecondly*, whether *the Audience be really entertain'd with immodeft Songs and Luft*; and *thirdly*, if they fhould happen to be in fuch a taking, whether it amounts to as great a Sin, as *doing Honour to the Devil, in the Name of fome Heathen God.*

To the *firft*, I can only fay that People of the beft
Breeding,

Breeding, the niceſt Taſte, and the moſt ſtrict Virtue do not apprehend *Impurity and Filthineſs to be generally in theſe Entertainments*, notwithſtanding this Author affirms it ſo roundly. To the *ſecond* (wherever the Author may have got his Information) the ſame good People are ready to aſſure him, that they neither are, nor ever go to be, *entertain'd with immodeſt Songs and Luſt*. And as to the *third* Particular, before I can determine any thing, I muſt conſider the Word *Luſt* a little, of which our Author makes ſo great a Uſe throughout his whole Treatiſe. *Luſt*, and *Paſſion*, and *Rant*, are the great Sins which he lays to the Charge of thoſe who go to Plays. Whereas *Luſt*, ſimply taken, can be no more a Sin than Hunger or Thirſt ; nor is it in any one's Power to prevent the one more than the others. They were certainly intended by our great Creator as a Means to continue and preſerve his Creatures upon Earth: And therefore, in themſelves, cannot be evil, unleſs they are abus'd to ill Purpoſes. They are neceſſary Appetites, and altogether innocent, as long as they crave after nothing but what is lawful: When they do otherwiſe, either one or t'other of them, they are criminal: As they are alſo, when abus'd to any Exceſs, even upon lawful Objects. Now, whoever have confeſs'd to our Author, that upon ſuch Occaſions they are inſpired with Luſt toward unlawful Objects, I grant it is ſinful in ſuch to go to Plays; and would adviſe them to ſtay away, till they have got rid of ſuch an irregular Appetite ; as I would alſo thoſe who are apt to be troubled with the like Infirmity at Church. As for *Paſſion*, I can't think it *a Sin* to be preſent while another Perſon is *really* tranſported with it; much leſs, when we know he is only feigning and repreſenting ſuch *Paſſion*. And then, as for *Rant*, I take it to be —— I don't know what; a ſort of Nonſenſe, which, like

a Chip in Porridge, can neither do neither Good nor
Hurt; nor consequently render any one *guilty* in hap-
pening to have the Drum of his Ear struck with it.
Therefore I leave the Reader to judge, whether simple
Lust, if any one should be overtaken with it; or
Passion, if one should chance to see it represented;
or *Rant*, if any one should be so unlucky as to hear
it, do singly, or all compounded together, amount
to *as great a Sin* as *doing Honour to the Devil in the
Name of some Heathen God.* As for his Particularity
in saying, *It is reasonable to think that the Play-houses
in this Kingdom are a greater Pleasure to the Devil*
than any where else, I take it to proceed from that
partial Affection to old *England*, which some People have been so ambitious of shewing, for these
last seven and thirty Years: For, if theatrical En-
tertaiments are the Worship of the Devil, the best
Judges will tell you he is better served at *Rome* and
Venice, nay even at *Paris*, than he is at *London*.

But, to proceed with our Author's *Reasoning*; af-
ter having affirmed several times over, without any
Proof, that going to a Play is going to worship the
Devil, says he (p. 15.) *Thus it is in the* Reason *of the
thing; and if we should now consider the State of our
Play-house, as it is in* Fact, *we should find it answering
all these Characters, and producing Effects suitable to its
Nature.* But *I shall forbear this Consideration, it being
as unnecessary to tell the Reader that our Play-house is in
Fact the Sink of Corruption and Debauchery; that it is
the general Rendezvous of the most profligate Persons of
both Sexes; that it corrupts the Air, and turns the adjacent Places into public Nusances; this is as unnecessary, as
to tell him that the Exchange is a Place of Merchandize.*

This Author is never farther from the Point
than when he talks of *Reasons* and *Facts*. That *the
Play house is the Rendezvous of the most profligate Persons of both Sexes*, I am ready to grant: But this is

an

an accidental Misfortune, lamented by the Generality of those that go to these Entertainments, and proceeding chiefly from the Negligence or perhaps Indulgence of those whom the Laws have appointed to remove and suppress such Irregularities. Suppose the Play-houses were no longer in being, and these profligate Persons should make our Churches their *Places of Rendezvous* (as, if they might be permitted, I make no Question but they would; and, as in *Spain* and *Portugal*, where they have not the Conveniences of Play-houses, they certainly do) must the Church be call'd the *House of the Devil* for this wicked, accidental Pollution of it, and be charg'd with *producing such bad Effects as suitable to its Nature?* No surely. Nor is there any more reason why the Play-house should. It is as unjustly charg'd with *corrupting the Air, and turning the adjacent Places into public Nusances.* In what Sense it is suppos'd to *corrupt the Air* I cannot imagine; but I conclude his *public Nusances* are the *profligate Persons* of the fair Sex, who are lodged thicker thereabouts than in any other Part of the Town; and this, I own, I should look upon as a Nusance, if I were obliged to be an Inhabitant amongst them. But, as there are in all great Cities some peculiar Places more frequently inhabited by People of this Sort, (as at *Rome* particularly, where they are tolerated upon paying an extraordinary Tax to the *Pope*) so in *London* they have chosen to make the Neighbourhood of the Play-houses their chief Residence: not that I believe there is a lewd Woman more upon Account of Play-houses subsisting; but, from the Remisness of the Constables and such Officers, they find these more convenient Places to carry on their Trade in, than any other; any Crowd or large Company being their proper Element. The Grievance therefore arising from the Swarming of such Vermin about

C

the

the Play-houses, is not owing to the Nature of Plays, but to the Neglect of those whose Concern it is to cleanse the Town upon such Occasions, and to sweep away all such licentious Associates from the Assemblies of People of the best Condition.

Yet our Author goes on after his usual manner, charging *first* the Play-houses, and *then* all those that ever go to them, with being the Cause and Encouragers of *Vice and Debauchery*, and of all those *Disorders* which are committed by the most profligate and abandon'd Part of Mankind.

But as these Disorders are not occasioned by the innocent and virtuous Part of the Audience, such ought, by no means, to be charged with the Consequences of them. *Totus Mundus agit Histrionem.* The World is a Comedy; in which there are many very vicious and wicked People, both Actors and Spectators: Must therefore the *innocent* go out of Life, because there are some *lewd* in it? There are *Pleasures and Entertainments* which are very innocent and inoffensive, and yet may happen to be, at the same time, *the Pleasures and Entertainments of the most debauch'd People:* Must therefore honest People *detest and abhor* all such Entertainments? Our Author says so: but forgets that, by the same Rule, they must forbear eating and drinking, and all the most necessary and innocently delightful Actions in Life.

However, our Author fancies all the World would be of his Opinion, if the contrary were not in Fashion. For he proceeds thus; *(p.* 17.) *As Prejudices, the Force of Education, the Authority of Number, the Way of the World, the Example of great Names may make People believe* (fancy they believe;) *so the same Causes may make People act against all Sense and Reason, and be guilty of Practices, which no more suit with the Purity of their Religion, than Transubstantiation agrees with common Sense.* This is very true; for Example,

ample, as great an Abfurdity as it is for an *Englifh*
Proteftant to defire *Popery* and the *Pretender*, I have
known fome, blinded by the Delufions aforefaid, *be-
lieve and act againft all Senfe and Reafon*, to fuch a
Degree, as to refufe Allegiance to our prefent moft
gracious Sovereign, and employ the utmoft of their
Power, their Wifhes, for a long Courfe of Years, in
Favour of both thefe; two the moft truly deteftable
Nufances in Life. But that People do *act againft all
Senfe and Reafon* in thinking Plays, in general, an
honeft laudable Diverfion, I deny, for the Reafons
I have before given; any more than they act againft
all Senfe and Reafon in going to Church: Since, in
both thefe Places, unregulated and neglected, very
great Immoralities may be practifed. Which is no
Reafon that either fhould be totally abandoned; but
only that which'ever of them ftands moft in need of
it, fhould be better difciplin'd and reform'd. I am
far from being an Advocate for Corruption and Debauchery any where, but am clear, that the Argument is as ftrong againft a Perfon's living in *London*,
becaufe the moft debauch'd and profligate Perfons
of both Sexes live there, as againft going to Plays
for that Reafon. I am for as much Reformation as
can conveniently be had, in our Diverfions, as well
as our Devotions, and wifh for it fincerely every
Day of my Life: But, in the mean time, I ftand a-
mazed to think how it can enter into the Head of
one who pretends to Reafon, that either Church or
Play-houfe, for want of fuch Reformation, fhould
be totally abolifh'd. None could ever defire the one
but a wicked harden'd *Atheift*; and I can give no
better a Name to him that endeavours the other,
than that of a dogmatical, querulous *Atheatrift*.

I fhall pafs over our Author's Inftance of *Trebonia*
(p. 18.) becaufe he owns *her Excufe may be allow'd
where the Diverfion is innocent:* and he has never yet

prov'd

prov'd that going to Plays is not fo. The Defign of Peoples going thither is to improve in moral Graces, and a laudable Behaviour in the World; as much as the Defign of going to Church is for Improvement in heavenly Grace and religious Virtues; and therefore, as I have demonftrated over and over, there is juft as much Reafon to forbear going to one as the other, becaufe wicked People come there, and you are fometimes entertain'd with Rant, Paffion, and Nonfenfe. If People go to either of thefe Places with an Intent to indulge themfelves in any criminal Defire, they certainly do a wrong thing; but if not, how is it poffible that the criminal Defires and Irregularities of others fhould be imputed to them?

P. 19. The Author, fpeaking of *Mafquerades*, fays, it is a *Diverfion new in our Country*. Now there are many Reafons to make one think it is a very old one. I don't remember to have read of them before Cardinal *Woolfey*'s time; tho' it is probable they were in Ufe long before. In the Reigns of the *Stuarts* they were very frequent. And tho' they were not in Vogue fome time after the *Revolution*; yet toward the latter End of Queen ANNE (when fome People were drunk at the imaginary Approach of *Popery* and *Slavery*) they were aufpicioufly reviv'd under the Adminiftration and Conduct of the Duke *D'Aumont*; and from that *Æra* we may date their prefent Continuance among us: Which, as has been already obferv'd by a moft worthy Prelate of our Church, is one good Reafon, among many others, why they fhould be hated and difcountenanc'd by all true Lovers of their Country. Yet, upon this Ground, I fufpect, it is that our Author fpeaks fo favourably of them, as to fay, there are *more and ftronger Reafons for a conftant Abhorrence of the Stage, than of Mafquerades.*

He

He is as much miſtaken (p. 20.) in his Inſtance of *Painting*; where he affirms that *Painting is a great Sin*; and takes it for granted that *the Uſe of Paint is always odious and ſinful*: And tho' he owns there is *no expreſs Text of Scripture againſt Painting*; yet he ſays *in judging according to Scripture*, People muſt *hold it as unreaſonable to paint ſometimes, as to be ſometimes malicious, indevout, proud, or falſe*. No ſure; it can never be right to be either malicious, indevout, proud, or falſe: But ſince it is no where forbidden in Scripture, where can be the Harm in painting *ſometimes*; provided it be done with a modeſt, and an humble Spirit, and for fear of appearing ſhockingly diſagreeable in the Eyes of our Fellow-Chriſtians? Why do People waſh their Faces and dreſs their Heads, but to look pleaſing and well upon each other: And why, for the ſame Reaſon, if the Nature of the thing requires it, ſhould they not add a little Varniſh to their Complexion; to make a ſallow Skin look freſh and lively; and to conceal from the World a Face ſo unfortunately deform'd with Freckles, that it reſembles the Belly of a Toad? Pray how comes *dying* the Face, only to make it more agreeable to the Spectators (for that I ſuppoſe to be the only Motive) to be a greater Sin than covering the reſt of the Body with ſuch a Variety of Dyes, as is generally the Faſhion? If this Affectation of Colours proceeds from a mere *Vanity of Mind and Fondneſs of Beauty*, as I ſuppoſe it moſt commonly does, muſt it be call'd a *great Sin* for that? In what part of Scripture, I pray, are *Vanity of Mind and Fondneſs of Beauty* ſtyl'd *great Sins?* And yet the Author's chief Ground for *condemning* Painting as a great Sin, is for its *proceeding from a Vanity of Mind only, and a Fondneſs of Beauty*. However, be it ſo, wearing colour'd Cloaths from the ſame Principles, muſt be equally as great a Sin: But where

neither

neither Face nor Body are cover'd with Colours, from any such wrong Motives, neither can be sinful. Yet our Author proceeds, (p. 21.) according to his usual Correctness, asserting that *Painting is contrary to Humility.* Whenever either *Painting* or *going to Plays* are us'd upon an ill Account, I shall be as ready to condemn them as he can be: but in the mean time, I affirm that both may be us'd, not only innocently, but to good Purposes. The Abuse of *Painting,* and of the *Stage* to ill Purposes, all reasonable People must abhor; but this is no reason why neither should ever be us'd at all; when one may be as innocently ornamental, as t'other may be innocently instructive.

But to proceed with him. (p. 22.) He says, *a polite Writer of a late Paper thought he had sufficiently ridicul'd a certain Lady's Pretensions to Piety; when, speaking of her Closet, he says,*

> *Together lie her Prayer-book and Paint,*
> *At once t'improve the Sinner and the Saint.*

Here again he has mistaken the Case; and introduc'd a Quotation at second hand, without knowing for what Purpose it was written, or quoted by the Author from whence he has taken it. This celebrated Couplet is Part of a Satyr, written by the late ingenious Earl of *Dorset,* to expose the Hypocrisy of a Woman who was a pretended Saint, but a real Sinner. Her using her *Prayer-book* for a Pretence to Piety, and her *Paint* for an Improvement in Sin, justly and equally make her the Subject of Satyr and Ridicule: they were both abus'd. Neither does Sir *Richard Steele,* the Author of that *Spectator,* (N° 79.) quote those Verses to any other Purpose than to expose those Ladies (not any *certain Lady*) who are so silly as to mix their Devotions with their Vanities,

Vanities, Dresses and Diversions. He does not pretend to shew that *Religion* and *Painting* are incompatible in the same Person, but only that the Exercise of them is inconsistent at the same Time. He thinks it does not look well to see the *Prayer-book and Paint* lie upon the same Table. He has not a single Word against mere *Painting* in that whole Paper: Tho' one would think, from what this Author says of him, that he had employ'd the best part of that *Spectator* in inveighing against it.

The Author, having compleated what he calls his Arguments, proceeds (p. 23.) and says, *I shall now make a Reflection or two upon the present celebrated Entertainment of the Stage, which is so much to the Taste of this Christian Country, that it has been acted almost every Night this whole Season, I mean* Apollo *and* Daphne. Now, tho' I am far from setting up for an Advocate of this *celebrated Entertainment*, knowing nothing of it indeed, but only that it pleases the Generality of People, and displeases our Author; yet I'll venture a Wager that we find him as much mistaken in his Reflections upon this in particular, as he has been in his Condemnation of Stage Entertainments in general.

He begins, p. 23. *The First Scene is said to be, a magnificent Palace discover'd:* Venus *attended with Graces and Pleasures. Now how is it possible that such a Scene as this should be fit for the Entertainment of Christians?* &c. *The very proposing such a Scene as this, supposes the Audience to be fit for the Entertainment of Lust and Wantonness. Can the Wit of Man invent any thing more contrary to our* Religion, *than an Entertainment from* Venus *attended with her Pleasures?* &c. *Such a Scene is much fitter to debauch a Christian Audience, than a Scene of Cursing and Blaspheming.* To this I answer, that simply to represent Venus *and her Pleasures* to the Eye, can be no more contrary to Religion, than barely naming them to the Ear

would

would be; there must be something immodest and shocking either in the Action or Discourse, to make either one or the other Offensive. I take Venus *and her Pleasures*, as here represented, to be as innocent as a Picture in which half a Dozen beautiful Women are figur'd, or as a History in which they are describ'd only. Yet one would think, by the Author's Account of this Matter, that the Person who represents this *Venus* was actually possess'd of a Secret Power (such as was attributed to the Heathen *Venus* of old) of inspiring People's Minds with amorous Sentiments: And not only so, but that her mere Presence could influence the Spectators to such a Degree, as to make them fall to embracing and enjoying each other upon the Spot. For what but such a Notion as this could make a Man so angry with a few mute Figures? and compare those that behold them *to the Idolaters of old?* What does all this raving amount to? Does any one worship these Deities among us? or look upon them to be any thing but mere Pageants? *Yet*, says our Author, *how are we more enlighten'd than* the Heathens of old, *if none of us considereth in his Heart, neither is there Knowledge nor Understanding in us to say, These are the filthy Deities of the Devil's Invention, with which he polluted and defil'd the Heathen World*; (Who supposes they are any thing else?) *and shall we still preserve their Power amongst us? Shall we make such Abominations our Diversion?* Yes surely; what should we make of them, but our sport and ridicule? What can we do better with such mock Deities, but laugh at them? and sometimes stare a little; and admire, how any People could ever be so stupid as to be serious in their Worship of them? Yet this poor Man supposes the Audience to be assembled together with great Sincerity, *to celebrate the Power of* Venus, as a real Goddess. Baal (says he) *is as fit for our Devotions,* as Venus *is for our Rejoicings and Praises.*

Praises. Nay he carries it so far as to say (p. 24.) that the very naming such a *Scene* as this is *unlawful Language,* and carries as great a *Contrariety* to our Religion as the *Worship* of Baal. At that rate, what has he been doing all this while, who has *nam'd* it so often? And indeed one may venture to affirm that the Generality of the Audience were no more inspir'd with *Lust* and *Wantonness* upon seeing this mock *Venus* and her *Pleasures,* than our Author was in Writing of them, and others will be in Reading of them.

But now he comes closer to the Point, and introduces *two Women* (*whom he supposes to be baptiz'd Christians*) *representing* Venus *and* Diana *in this Language,*

> Ven. *Amorous Kisses,*
> Dian. *Nuptial Blisses,*
> { *Lover's Pleasures,*
> { *Cupid's Treasures,*
> { *Are the Sweets that Life improve.*

This he imagines to be such obscene Language as to be fit for none to hear but *Rakes* and *Prostitutes.* Why so, I pray? does not every one know that the *Pleasures of Love* are really and truly very *sweet,* and very great *Improvers* of the Happiness of Life, and may, at the same time, be very innocent? Are not *nuptial Blisses* very honest allowable Delights? And are not *amorous kisses* known to be a Part of them? These jingling Words contain no more than what the Audience all knew before ever they heard them sung there. That *Love's a sweet Pleasure* is one of the most notorious Maxims in Life; as well as, that *Pleasure* is the most desireable Thing in Nature. *The Ways of Wisdom are Ways of Pleasantness.* Nor are Pleasures ever the less worthy Objects of a Wise

Man's

Man's Pursuit, because Rakes and Fools will take
unlawful Ways to come at them. One would think
the Author of these Rhymes had sufficiently guarded
against any sinister Interpretation of the *Blisses* he
speaks of, by calling them *nuptial*; yet our candid
ingenuous Author is resolv'd to forget this, and calls
it *singing the Praises of Debauchery*, (p. 25.) and *hearing the Praises of Lewdness*. But he makes me laugh,
to see him so seriously supposing that all this ridiculous Mockery is a direct and real Worship of the
antiquated Goddess *Venus*. *No Christian* (says he)
need be told that Venus *and her* Graces *are as much the
Devil's Machinery, as Witches and Imps*. I will suppose, for once, there were actually existing such Things
as Venus *and her* Graces, *Witches and Imps*, present-
ing themselves to the View of a great Number of
Spectators, and singing what you please; would it
be impossible for these Spectators to preserve their
Christian Purity of Heart all the while? Is it any
ways necessary that they should relish and entertain
the same Sentiments, which are contain'd in such
Songs? Nothing like it. But here the Case is otherwise. A poor mean Mortal, known to all the Spectators to be such, personates a Goddess, worship'd
by the Heathens of old with such a Worship, as
these Spectators are convinc'd was false, ridiculous
and immodest. This poor Mortal affirms in a Song,
that the *Pleasures of Love are sweet*; without giving
the least hint that she means unlawful Love; (the
contrary being directly express'd.) And yet our Author accuses *her* for inspiring, and the Audience for
being inspir'd with, *Lust, Lewdness*, and *Debauchery*;
and tells them they are no better than a Parcel of
Rakes and *Prostitutes* for being present at such an Entertainment. I think it proper, upon this Occasion,
to put our Author in Mind, that the Ancients did
not always understand the Word *Venus*, by which
they

they exprefs'd the Attribute of Beauty, in a bad Senfe, fo as to intend fomething lafcivious, but very often in a modeft and a good one. Hence are derived the Words *venuftas, veneror, veneratio,* applied by them, and by us us'd, to exprefs that Regard which is claim'd by the moft defervedly amiable and divine Objects.

The other Jingle, upon which he falls fo outragioufly (p. 26.) is fo much of the fame Nature with the foregoing, that all the fame may well be faid in Defence of it. The Nature of fuch Ballads, when the worft is faid of them that can be, is that they have a Tendency to excite kind Inclinations in the Breafts of amorous People, toward the Objects of their Love: which, when fuch Love is plac'd where it ought to be, is far enough from being an ill Office. And, if it happens to be wrong placed, that cannot be imputed to the chinking of a few infipid Words, but flows from the irregular cravings of an ungovern'd Paffion; fuch as incontinent People do not catch in this or that particular Place, but carry about with them where-ever they go.

Our Author next falls very heavily upon *Bacchus, Pan,* and *Silenus,* attended with *Satyrs, Fawns,* and *Silvans*; and asks, *what have Chriftians to do with this Company?* I anfwer; to laugh at them; to wonder how the Heathen World could be funk fo low in Stupidity, as ever to make fuch ridiculous Beings the Objects of their religious Worfhip; and, in the Joy of their Hearts, to thank God that they know better. Yet our Author goes on upon his old falfe *Hypothefis,* concluding the Audience is affembled together out of a religious Refpect to thefe whimfical *Chimeras,* and are as much prejudic'd in favour of their Divinity, as the Heathens of old were. *If this is not being at the Devil's Table,* (fays he) *he had no Table in the Heathen World.* If it is, then our

Author,

Author, and all that ever taught and learn'd the History of these Demi-Gods, have been at *the Devil's Table* likewise. For what is this more than a bare Character of their Persons presented to our View, with their proper Symbols and Ornaments, in somewhat a more lively Manner than it is done by Father *Montfaucon*, in his *Antiquity Explain'd*. The Attributes of these impure Deities are indeed describ'd by some sort of Action upon the Stage, but not acted in reality; tho' our Author argues upon a Supposition that they are. To hear and see these shadowy Descriptions, he says, is as great a Sin as *making a Jest of the Sacraments*. (p. 27.) *It may be* (says he) *you could not sit in the Play-house, if you saw Baptism made a Jest of, and it's Use reproach'd*. No certainly; but sure a Christian may sit there, properly enough, to see Heathenism, with all its Rites and Ceremonies, made a Jest of.

To p. 30. he goes on begging the Question, as usual, and supposing that the Audience give their Money to the Players, purely to be criminal and wicked upon the Stage: which is all Mistake. For tho' *Venus*, and *Silenus, talk* like themselves, yet, I presume, they act nothing shocking to the most modest Eyes. And what does this amount to, more than such a Description of their Natures, as is to be met with in the Antient Mythology? Such as the Fathers of old, not only read, but have written so much about; and that in Language a thousand times more obscene, than ever was utter'd in the Play-house: Such as the most grave and learned Divines in all ages have been conversant with, and such as is daily inculcated into our Youth of the best Condition, as the only Means of attaining a polite Education. Yet, to be a Spectator at a Representation of this very thing, our Author calls *serving the Devil*; and says, *If there be any certain Marks of the*

Devil's

Devil's Power, or Presence, in any Assemblies, Places, or Temples of the Heathen World, the same are as certain Marks of his Power and Presence in our Play-house.

The Author having done with his Reflections and Arguments, proceeds to apply them in the Cases of *Levis*, *Jucunda*, &c. But, as all this is grounded upon his mistaken Supposition, that the Players do really commit all those Sins which they only Paint out and Characterise upon the Stage, and that therefore it is absolutely unlawful to go to Plays, I shall pass it over without any farther Remarks; leaving it to the Reader's Judgment, whether, as I have stated the Case, it may not be as innocent to go to a Play, as to any other Recreation.

As to his Quotation out of Archbishop *Tillotson*, (p. 38.) which he tells us he produces *for no other End, but to prevent the Charge of Uncharitableness*; I must assure him that it will by no means serve him to that End. The Archbishop is far enough from decrying Plays in *general*; he only particularizes, *As Plays are now order'd, As now the Stage is*, &c. The notoriously debauch'd Reigns of *Charles* and *James* the Seconds, (when Profaneness was the Wit, and Lewdness the Gallantry of the Court) very naturally drew the Stage into the same vicious Taste; and this was what so justly provok'd the Zeal of that good Archbishop. He, no where, condemns Theatrical Performances in *general*; nor says, it is impossible that Players can be Christians; as our Author so frequently has done: and for which, the Use of this great Name will never clear him from the Charge of Uncharitableness.

The Clergy of the true Church (as they affect to call themselves) in the two Reigns beforemention'd, were too loyal to make much bustle about the Immorality of the Stage, for fear they should give a Handle

to

to Men of Republican Principles forsooth, to impute the Iniquity of the Times to the Influence of the Court; so they, very discretely, waited till after the *Revolution*: When Mr. *Rowe*'s honest Tragedy of *Tamerlane*, form'd upon the Plan of Liberty, gave the Reverend Mr. *Collier* such a Disgust to the Stage, that he was convinc'd its *Vices* and *Immoralities* were no longer to be born. The Comedy call'd *the Non-juror*, which so justly and wittily exposes the wretched Schemes of that absurd Sect, extorted a *Serious Remonstrance* from the Reverend Mr. *Bedford*; And, the best of our Plays, being frequently honour'd and encourag'd by the Presence of the Royal Family, as well as the most honourable and worthy of the King's Subjects, out steps the Reverend Mr. *Law*, and undertakes *fully to demonstrate the absolute Unlawfulness of the Stage-Entertainment*: which he does; *First*, by affirming very positively and roundly, that the Play-house is the Temple of the Devil; *Secondly*, by asserting very charitably and dogmatically, that the Players are actually guilty of all that Villany and Wickedness which they there represent; and *Thirdly*, by concluding very respectfully and civilly, that all who go to see them, without Exception, are at least as guilty; by being Partakers in and Promoters of such a Complication of abominable and detestable Sins. For (p. 37.) he has these Words, *The Use and Encouragement of the Stage, is a deliberate, continued, open and public Declaration in favour of Lewdness, Immorality and Prophaneness.* The Insinuation that is couch'd in such a bold but groundless Allegation as this, must be obvious to every honest Mind.

That there are in some Plays things Scandalous and Offensive, I am ready to grant; and should be glad to see them so distinguish'd, by a judicious impartial Hand, as to bring those Plays into Disuse,

'till

'till the offending Parts should be left out of them.
But that Plays in general, and especially Representations of the Heathen Gods, in the ludicrous Way
in which we represent them, are sinful and antichri-
stian, I can by no Means agree; without condemning the Fathers, our two famous Universities, all
Schools and Nurseries of Learning, the best Authors Ancient and Modern, and all the Christian
Churches in the Universe. And therefore, tho' I
am as much for the Reformation of the Stage
from all the Irregularities and Abuses of it, as
the most strict Advocate for the Honour of our
Holy Religion can be, yet, for the Reasons beforemention'd, I cannot think a total Abolition of it
would be right; or indeed so much as Practicable.

And thus I have complied with our Author in
what he thinks (p. 50.) *reasonable People* ought *to
do in this Case.* As I cannot see, much less *yield
to, the Truth of his Arguments,* whereby he pretends
to have prov'd that *the Use of the Stage is certainly to be reckon'd among great and flagrant Sins ;* I
have answer'd them; and given my Reasons for the
contrary Opinion; in a Manner however Slight and
Hasty, yet I hope sufficient to keep the Minds of
the Tender and Innocent from being drawn into
a mistaken Apprehension of Guilt; to preserve the
noble and instructive Diversion of Stage-Entertainments, well regulated, from being totally banish'd
and exploded; and, in the mean Time, to prevail
with those who have no Taste for such Pleasures
themselves, to judge charitably of others; who innocently, both in the Intention and Consequence,
make such Entertainments the Amusement of their
Leisure Hours.

F I N I S.

THE
ENTERTAINMENT
OF THE
STAGE,

A

Corrupt and Sinful Entertainment,

CONTRARY

To the whole Nature of Christian
Piety, and constantly to be avoided by all sincere Christians.

EDINBURGH,
Printed by Mr. JAMES DAVIDSON and COM-
PANY, and sold at the said Mr. *Davidson's*
Shop, and other Booksellers in Town, 1727.

ADVERTISEMENT.

Have only one *Thing* to desire of the Reader, *Not that he would like and approve of these Reflections, but that he will not suffer himself to dislike or condemn them, till he has put his Arguments into Form, and knows how many Doctrines of Scripture he can* bring against those *Things that I have asserted. So far as he can shew that I have reasoned wrong, or mistook the Doctrine of Scripture, so far he has a Right to censure. But* general Dislikes *are mere* Tempers, *as blind as* Passions, *and are always the strongest where Reasons are most wanted. If People will dislike because they will, and condemn Doctrines, only because it suits better with their* Tempers and Practices, *than to consider and understand them to be true ; they act by the same Spirit of* Popery, *as is most remarkable in the lowest Bigots, who are resolute in a general Dislike of all* Protestant *Doctrines, without suffering themselves to consider and understand upon what* Truth *they are founded.*

The ENTERTAINMENT *of the* STAGE, *is a corrupt and sinful Entertainment,* &c.

 HAVE shewn you elfe-
where, that the reading
of *Plays,* or any other
Books of that kind, is a
dangerous and finful En-
tertainment, that corrupts
our Hearts, and feparates
the Holy Spirit from us.
You will now perhaps ask
me, if it is unlawful for a
Chriftian to go to the *Play-houfe.* I anfwer, that
it is abfolutely unlawful. As unlawful, as for a
Chriftian to be a *Drunkard,* or a *Glutton,* or to *Curfe*
and *Swear.* This I think will be eafily prov'd.

FOR let us confider the Doctrine of the Apoftle,
we are abfolutely forbid all *corrupt Communication,*
and for this important Reafon, becaufe it *grieves*
and

and *separates* the Holy Spirit from us. Is it unlawful therefore to have any *corrupt Communication* of our own? And can we think it *lawful* to go *to Places set apart* for that Purpose? To give our Money, and *hire* Persons to corrupt our Hearts with ill Discourses, and inflame all the disorderly Passions of our Nature? We have the Authority of Scripture to affirm, That *evil Communication corrupts good Manners*; and that *unedifying Discourses grieve the Holy Spirit*. Now the *third* Commandment is not more plain and express against *Swearing*, than this Doctrine is plain and positive against going to the *Play-house*. If you should see a Person, that acknowledges the *third* Commandment to be a Divine Prohibition against *Swearing*, yet going to a *House*, and giving his *Money* to Persons, who were there met, to *Curse* and *Swear* in fine Language, and invent *musical Oaths* and *Imprecations*, would you not think him Mad in the highest Degree? Now consider, whether there be a less Degree of Madness in going to the *Play-house*. You own, that God has called you to a great Purity of Conversation, that you are forbid all *foolish Discourse*, and *filthy Jestings*, as expresly, as you are forbid *Swearing*; that you are to let no *corrupt Communication* proceed out of your Mouth, but *such as is good for the Use of edifying*; and yet you go to the *House set apart* for corrupt Communications, you hire Persons to entertain you with all manner of *Ribbaldry*, *Prophaness*, *Rant*, and *Impurity* of Discourse; who are to present you with *vile* Thoughts, and *lewd* Imaginations in *fine Language*, and to make *wicked*, *vain*, and *impure* Discourse, more lively and affecting, than you could possibly have it in any ill Company. Now, is not this sinning with as high a Hand, and

as

as grosly offending, against the plain Doctrines of Scripture, as if you was to give your *Money* to be entertained with *mufical Oaths* and *Curfes* ? You might reafonably think that *Woman* very ridiculous in her *Piety*; that durft not Swear herself, but fhould neverthelefs frequent *Places* to hear *Oaths*. But you may as juftly think her very ridiculous in her *Mode-fty*, who, tho' fhe dares not to fay, or look, or do an immodeft Thing her felf, fhall yet give her *Mo-ney*, to fee *Women* forget the *Modefty* of their Sex, and talk *impudently* in a publick *Play-houfe*. If the *Play-houfe* was fill'd with *Rakes* and ill *Women*, there would be nothing to be wonder'd at in fuch an Affembly ; for *fuch Perfons* to be delighted with fuch Entertainments, is as natural, as for any *A-nimal* to delight in its proper *Element*. But for Per-fons who profefs Purity and Holinefs, who would not be fufpected of *Immodefty* or *corrupt Communica-tion*, for them to come under the Roof of a *Houfe devoted* to fuch ill Purpofes, and be pleas'd Specta-tors of fuch Actions and Difcourfes, as are the Plea-fure of the moft abandon'd Perfons ; for them to give their Money to be thus entertain'd, is fuch a Contradiction to all Piety and common Senfe, as cannot be fufficiently expos'd.

AGAIN, when you fee the *Players* acting with Life and Spirit, Men and Women *equally bold* in all Inftances of *Prophanefs*, *Paffion*, and *Immodefty*, I dare fay, you never fufpect any of them to be Per-fons of *Chriftian Piety*. You can't even in your I-magination join Piety to fuch Manners, and fuch a Way of Life. Your Mind will no more allow you to join Piety with the Behaviour of the *Stage*, than it will allow you to think *two* and *two* to be *ten*. And perhaps you had rather fee your Son chain'd

to

to a *Galley*, or your Daughter driving *Plows*, than getting their Bread on the *Stage*, by administring in so scandalous a Manner to the Vices and corrupt Pleasures of the World. Let this therefore be another Argument to prove the *absolute Unlawfulness* of going to a *Play*. For consider with your self, is the Business of *Players* so contrary to Piety, so inconsistent with the Spirit and Temper of a true Christian, that it is next to a Contradiction to suppose them united? How then can you take your self to be *Innocent*, who *delight* in their Sins, and *hire* them to commit them? You may make your self a Partaker of other Men's Sins, by Negligence, and for want of reproving them; but certainly, if you stand by, and assist Men in their Evil Actions, if you make their Vices your Pleasure and Entertainment, and pay your Money to be so entertained, you make your self a Partaker of their Sins in a very high Degree. And consequently it must be as unlawful to go to a *Play*, as it is unlawful to approve, encourage, assist, and reward a Man for renouncing a Christian Life. Let therefore every *Man* or *Woman* that goes to a *Play*, ask themselves this Question, Whether it suits with their Religion, to act the *Parts* that are there acted? Perhaps they would think this as inconsistent with that Degree of Piety that they profess, as to do the vilest Things. But let them consider, that it must be a wicked and unlawful Pleasure, to delight in any Thing that they dare not do themselves. Let them also consider, that they are really *acting* those Indecencies and Impieties themselves, which they think is the particular Guilt of the *Players*. For a Person may very justly be said to do that *himself*, which he *pays* for the doing, and which is done for his Pleasure.

You

You must therefore, if you would be confistent with your self, as much abhor the Thoughts of being at a *Play*, as of being a *Player* your self; for to think that you must forbear the one and not the other, is as absurd, as to suppose, that you must be temperate your self, but may assist, encourage, and reward other People for their Intemperance. The Business of a *Player* is prophane, wicked, lewd, and immodest, to be any Way therefore approving, assisting, or encouraging him in such a Way of Life, is as evidently sinful, as 'tis sinful to assist and encourage a Man in *Stealing*, or any other Wickedness.

To proceed. When I consider *Churches*, and the Matter of *Divine Service*, that it consists of holy Readings, Prayers, and Exhortations to Piety, there is Reason to think, that the House of God is a natural Means of promoting Piety, and Religion, and rendering Men devout and sensible of their Duty to God. The very Nature of Divine Assemblies, thus carried on, has this direct Tendency. I ask you whether this is not very plain, that *Churches* thus employed should have this Effect.

Consider therefore the *Play-house*, and the Matter of the Entertainment there, as it consists of *Love-intreagues*, *blasphemous Passions*, *prophane Discourses*, *lewd Descriptions*, *filthy Jests*, and all the most extravagant Rant of wanton, vile, profligate Persons of both Sexes, heating and inflaming one another with all the *Wantonness* of Address, the *Immodesty* of Motion, and *Lewdness* of Thought, that Wit can invent; consider, I say, whether it be not plain, that a House so employed, is as certainly serving the Cause of *Immorality* and *Vice*, as the House of God is serving the Cause of *Piety*? For what is there in our *Church-Service*, that shews it

B   to

to be *useful* to Piety and Holiness? What is there in Divine Worship to correct and amend the Heart, but what is directly *contrary* to all that is doing in the *Play-house?* So that one may with the same Assurance affirm, that the *Play-house*, not only when some very prophane Play is on the *Stage*, but in its *daily, common* Entertainment, is as certainly the *House of the Devil*, as the Church is the *House of God.* For though the Devil be not professedly worshipped by Hymns directed to him, yet most that is there Sung is to his Service, he is there *obeyed* and *pleased* in as certain a Manner, as God is Worshipped and Honoured in the Church.

You must easily see, that this Charge against the *Play-house*, is not the Effect of any *particular Temper*, or *Weakness* of Mind, that it is not an *uncertain Conjecture*, or *religious Whimsy*, but is a Judgment founded as plainly in the *Nature* and *Reason* of Things, as when it is affirmed that the House of God is of Service to Religion. And he that absolutely condemns the *Play-house*, as wicked and corrupting, proceeds upon as much Truth and Certainty, as he that absolutely commends the *House of God*, as Holy, and tending to promote Piety.

When therefore any one pretends to vindicate the *Stage* to you, as a proper Entertainment for holy and religious Persons, you ought to reject the Attempt with as much Abhorrence, as if he should offer to shew you, that our *Church-Service* was rightly formed for those Persons to join in, who are *devoted to the Devil.* For to talk of the *Lawfulness* and *Usefulness* of the *Stage* is fully as absurd, as contrary to the plain Nature of Things, as to talk of the *Unlawfulness* and *Mischief* of the Service of the Church. He therefore that tells you, that you may

safely

safely go to the *Play-house*, as an innocent, useful Entertainment of your Mind, commits the same Offence, against common Sense, as if he should tell you, that it was dangerous to attend at Divine Service, and that its *Prayers* and *Praises* were great *Pollutions* of the Mind.

FOR the Matter and Manner of *Stage-entertainments*, is as undeniable a Proof, and as obvious to common Sense, that the House belongs to the Devil, and is the Place of his Honour, as the Matter and Manner of *Church-Service* proves that the Place is appropriated to God.

OBSERVE therefore, that as you do not want the Assistance of any one, to shew you the *Usefulness* and *Advantage* of Divine Service, because the Thing is plain, and speaks for itself. So neither, on the other Hand, need you any one to shew you the *Unlawfulness* and *Mischief* of the Stage, because there the Thing is equally plain, and speaks for itself. So that you are to consider your self, as having the same Assurance that the *Stage* is wicked, and to be abhorred and avoided by all Christians, as you have that the Service of the Church is Holy, and to be sought after by all Lovers of Holiness. Consider therefore, that your Conduct, with Relation to the *Stage*, is not a Matter of *Nicety* or *scrupulous Exactness*, but that you are as certain that you do Wrong in as notorious a Manner, when you go to the *Play-house*, as you are certain that you do Right, when you go to *Church*.

NOW it is of mighty Use to conceive Things in a right Manner, and to see them as they are in their own Nature. While you consider the *Play-house*, as only a *Place of Diversion*, it may perhaps give no Offence to your Mind : There is nothing *shocking* in

the

the Thought of It : but, if you would lay aside this Name of it for a while, and consider it in its *own Nature*, as it really is, you will find that you are as much deceived, if you consider the *Play-house*, as only a *Place of Diversion*, as you would be, if you considered the House of God only as a *Place of Labour*.

When therefore you are tempted to go to a *Play*, either from your own Inclination, or the Desire of a Friend, fancy that you was asked in plain Terms to go to the Place of the *Devil's Abode*, where he holds his *filthy Court* of evil Spirits; that you was asked to join in an Entertainment, where he was at the *Head* of it, where the whole of it was in order to his Glory, that Men's Hearts and Minds might be separated from God, and plunged into all the Pollutions of Sin and Brutality. Fancy that you was going to a Place that as certainly belongs to the Devil, as the *Heathen Temples* of old, where *Brutes* were worshipped, where *wanton Hymns* were Sung to *Venus*, and *drunken Songs* to the God of *Wine*. Fancy that you was as certainly going to the Devil's Triumph, as if you was going to those *old Sports*, where People committed Murder, and offered Christians to be devoured by wild Beasts, for the Diversion of Spectators. Now whilst you consider the *Play-house* in this View, I suppose that you can no more go to a *Play*, than you can expresly renounce your Christianity.

Consider therefore now, that you have not been frighting your self with *groundless Imaginations*, but that what you have here fancied of the *Play-house* is as strictly true, as if you had been fancying, that when you go to Church, you go into the House of God, where the heavenly Host attend upon his Service;

vice: and that when you there read the Scriptures, and sing holy Praises, you join with the Quires above, and do God's Will on Earth as it is done in Heaven. For observe, I pray you, how justly that Opinion of the *Play-house* is founded. For, was it a Joy and Delight to the Devil to see *Idols worshipp'd*, to see Hymns and Adorations offer'd up to impure and filthy Deities? Were Places and Festivals appointed for such Ends, justly esteem'd Places and Festivals devoted to the Devil? Now give the Reason why all this was justly reckoned a Service to the Devil, and you will give as good a Reason, why the *Play-house* is to be esteemed his *Temple*. For, what though Hymns and Adorations are not offered to impure and filthy Deities, yet if *Impurity* and *Filthiness* is there the *Entertainment*, if immodest Songs, prophane Rant, if Lust and Passion entertain the Audience, the Business is the same, and the Assembly does the *same Honour* to the Devil, though they are not gathered together in the Name of some *Heathen God*.

For Impurity and Prophaness, in the Worshippers of the true God, is as acceptable a Service to the Devil, as Impurity and Prophaness in any Idolaters, and perhaps a *lewd Song* in an Assembly of Christians gives him greater Delight, than if it had been sung in a Congregation of *Heathens*.

If therefore we may justly say, that a *House or Festival* was the Devil's, because he was *delighted* with it, because what was there done, was an *acceptable* Service to him, we may be assured that the *Play-house* is as really the House of the Devil, as any other House ever was. Nay, it is reasonable to think that the *Play-houses* in this Kingdom are a greater Pleasure to him than any *Temple* he ever had in the *Heathen World*. For as it is a greater Conquest to make the Disciples of Christ delight in *Lewdness* and *Prophaness*, than ignorant Heathens, so a *House*, that in the Midst of *Christian Churches*, trains up Christians in *Lewdness* and *Prophaness*, that makes the Worshippers of Christ flock together in Crowds to rejoice in an Entertainment, that is as contrary to the Spirit of Christ, as *Hell* is contrary to *Heaven*, a House so employed may justly be reckoned a more delightful Habitation of the Devil, than any Temple in the Heathen World. When therefore you go to the *Play-house*, you have as much Assurance, that you go to the Devil's peculiar Habitation, that you submit to his Designs, and rejoice in his Diversions, (which are his best Devices against Christianity) you have as must Assurance of this, as that they who worshipped filthy Deities, were in reality Worshippers of the Devil.

AGAIN, Consider those *old Sports* and *Diversions*, where Christians were sometimes thrown to wild Beasts, consider why such Sports might well be looked upon as the *Devil's Triumph*. I suppose you are at no Stand with your self, whether you should impute such Entertainments to the Devil: Consider therefore, why you should not as readily allow the *Stage* to be his Entertainment.

FOR was it a Delight to the Devil to see Heathens sporting with the bodily Death of Christians? And must it not be a greater Delight to him to see Christians sporting themselves in the Death of their Souls?

THE Heathens could only kill the Body, and separate it from the Soul, but these Christian-Diversions murder the Soul, and separate it from God. I dare say, no Arguments could convince you, that

it

it was *lawful* to rejoice at thofe Sports, which were thus defiled with human Blood ; but then pray remember, that if the Death of the Soul be as great a Cruelty, as the Death of the Body, if it be as dreadful for a Soul to be feparated from God, as to be feparated from the Body, you ought to think it as entirely unlawful to enter that Houfe, where fo many eternal Lives are facrificed, or ever to partake of thofe Diverfions which feparate fuch Numbers of Souls from God.

HENCE it appears, that if inftead of confidering the *Play-houfe*, as only a Place of Diverfion, you will but examine what Materials it is made of ; if you will but confider the Nature of the Entertainment, and what is there doing, you will find it as wicked a Place, as finful a Diverfion, and as truly the peculiar Pleafure and Triumph of the Devil, as any wicked . Place, or finful Diverfion, in the Heathen World. When therefore you are ask'd to go to a *Play*, don't think that you are ask'd only to go to a *Diverfion*, but be affured that you are ask'd to *yield* to the Devil, to go over to his *Party*, and to make one of his Congregation ; that if you do go, you have not only the Guilt of *buying* fo much vain and corrupt Communication, but are alfo as certainly guilty of going to the Devil's Houfe, and doing him the fame Honour, as if you was to partake of fome *Heathen Feftival.*

YOU muft confider, that all the Laughter there, is not only vain and foolifh, but that it is a Laughter amongft Devils, that you are upon *prophane Ground*, and hearing Mufick in the very Porch of Hell,

THUS it is in the Reafon of the Thing, and if we fhould now confider the State of our *Play-houfe*

as

as it is in Fact, we should find it answering all these Characters, and producing Effects suitable to its Nature: But I shall forbear this Consideration, it being as unnecessary to tell the Reader that our *Play-house* is in Fact the *Sink of Corruption and Debauchery*, that it is the general Rendezvouze of the most profligate Persons of both Sexes, that it corrupts the Air, and turns the adjacent Places into publick Nusances; this is as unnecessary, as to tell him, that the *Exchange* is a Place of *Merchandize.*

Now it is to be observed, that this is not the State of the *Play-house*, through any accidental Abuse, as any innocent or good Thing may be abused; but that Corruption and Debauchery, are the truely natural and genuine Effects of the *Stage-Entertainment*. Let not therefore any one say, that he is not answerable for those Vices and Debaucheries, which are occasioned by the *Play-house*, for so far as he partakes of the Pleasure of the *Stage*, and is an Encourager of it, so far he is chargeable with those Disorders which necessarily are occasioned by it. If Evil arises from our doing our Duty, or our Attendance at any *good Design*, we are to not to be frighted at it; but if Evil arises from any thing as its *natural* and *genuine* Effect, in all such Cases, so far as we conttibute to the Cause, so far we make our selves guilty of the Effects. So that all who any way assist the *Play-house*, or ever encourage it by their Presence, make themselves chargeable in some Degree, with all the Evils and Vices, which follow from it. Since therefore it cannot be doubted by any one, whether the *Play-house* be a Nursery of Vice and Debauchery, since the evil Effects it has upon People's Manners, is as visible as the Sun at Noon, one would imagine, that all People of Virtue

and

and Modefty, fhould not only avoid it, but avoid it with the utmoft Abhorrence; that they fhould be fo far from entering into it, that they fhould deteft the very Sight of it. For what a Contradiction is it to common Senfe, to hear a Woman lamenting the miferable Lewdnefs and Debauchery of the Age, the vicious Tafte, and irregular Pleafures of the World, and at the fame time dreffing her felf to meet the lewdeft Part of the World, at the Fountain-Head of all -Lewdnefs, and making her felf one of that Crowd, where every abandon'd Wretch is glad to be prefent? She may fancy that fhe hates and abominates their Vices, but fhe may depend upon it, that till fhe hates and abominates the Place of vicious Pleafures, till fhe dare not come near an Entertainment which is the Caufe of fo great Debauchery, and the Pleafure of the moft debauched People, till fhe is thus difpofed, fhe wants the trueft Sign of a real and Religious Abhorrence of the Vices of the Age.

For, to wave all other Confiderations, I would only ask her a Queftion or two on the fingle Article of *Modefty*. What is Modefty? Is it a little *mechanical outfide* Behaviour, that goes no farther than a few *Forms and Modes* at particular Times and Places? Or is it a *real Temper*, a rational Difpofition of the Heart, that is founded in *Religion*? Now if Modefty is only a mechanical Obfervance of a little outfide Behaviour, then I can eafily perceive how a modeft Woman may frequent *Plays*; there is no Inconfiftency for fuch a one to be one Thing in one Place, and another in another Place, to difdain an immodeft Converfation, and yet at the fame time relifh and delight in immodeft and impudent Speeches in a publick *Play-boufe*. But if

C

Mo-

Modesty is a *real Temper* and Disposition of the Heart, that is founded in the Principles of Religion, then I confess, I cannot comprehend how a Person of such Modesty, should ever come twice into a *Play-house.* For if it is Reason and Religion that has inspired her with a Modest Heart, that makes her careful of her Behaviour, that makes her hate and abhore every Word, or Look, or Hint, in Conversation, that has the Appearance of Lewdness, that makes her shun the Company of such as talk with too much Freedom ; if she is thus modest in *common Life*, from a Principle of Religion, a Temper of Heart, is it possible for such a one (I don't say to seek) but to bear with the Immodesty and Impudence of the *Stage ?* For must not Immodesty and Impudence, must not loose and wanton Discourse be the same *hateful Things*, and give the same Offence to a modest Mind, in one Place, as in another ? And must not that Place, which is the Seat of Immodesty, where Men and Women are trained up in Lewdness, where almost every Day in the Year, is a Day devoted to the Foolish Representations of *Rant, Lust*, and *Passion* ; must not such a Place, of all others, be the most odious to a Mind that is *truly Modest* upon Principles of *Reason and Religion ?* One would suppose, that such a Person should as much abominate the Place, as any other filthy Sight, and be as much offended with an Invitation to it, as if she was invited to see an immodest Picture. For the Representations of the *Stage*, the inflamed Passions of Lovers there described, are as gross an Offence to the Ear, as any Representation that can offend the Eye.

It ought not to be concluded, that because I affirm the *Play-house* to be an Entertaiment *contray*

to

to Modesty, that therefore I accuse all People as void
of Modesty, who ever go to it. I might affirm,
that *Transubstantiation* is contrary to all *Sense* and
Reason; but then it would be a wrong Conclusion
to say, that I affirmed that all who believe it are
void of all Sense and Reason. Now as *Prejudices*,
the Force of *Education*, the Authority of *Numbers*,
the Way of *World*, the Example of *great Names*,
may make People *believe*, so the same Causes may
make People *act* against *all Sense and Reason*, and
be guilty of Practices which no more suit with the
Purity of their Religion, than *Transubstantiation* a-
grees with *common Sense*.

To proceed. I once heard a young Lady thus
excusing her self for going to the *Play house*, that
she went but seldom, and then in Company of her
Mother and her *Aunt*, that they always knew their
Play before-hand, and never went on the *Sacrament-
Week*. And what Harm, pray, says she, can there
be in this ? It breaks in upon no Rules of my
Life, I neglect no Part of my Duty, I go to *Church*,
and perform the same Devotions at Home, as on
other Days. It ought to be observed, that this
Excuse can only be allowed where the *Diversion* it
self is *innocent*; it must therefore be first considered,
what the Entertainment is in it self, whether it be
suitable to the Spirit and Temper of Religion ; for
if it is right and proper in it self it needs no Excuse ;
but if it be *wrong* and *dangerous* to Religion, we
are not to use it *cautiously*, but avoid it *constantly*.

Secondly, It is no Proof of the Innocency of a
Thing, that it does not interfere with our *Hours of
Duty*, nor break the Regularity of our Lives, for
very wicked Ways of spending Time, may yet be
consistent with a regular Distribution of our Hours.

She

She muſt therefore conſider, not only whether ſuch a Diverſion hinders the Regularity of her Life, or breaks in upon her Devotions, publick or private, but whether it hinders or any way affects that *Spirit and Temper*, which all her Devotions aſpire after. Is it conformable to that Heavenly Affection, that Love of God, that Purity of Heart, that Wiſdom of Mind, that Perfection of Holineſs, that Contempt of the World, that Watchfulneſs and Selfdenial, that Humility and Fear of Sin ? Is it conformable to theſe Graces, which are to be the *daily Subject* of all her Prayers ? This is the only Way for her to know the *Innocency* of going to Play. If what ſhe there hears and ſees, has no *Contrariety* to any *Graces* or *Virtues* which ſhe prays for, if all that there paſſes be fit for the Purity and Piety of one that is led by the Spirit of Chriſt, and is working out her Salvation *with Fear and Trembling*, if the *Stage* be an Entertainment, that may be thought according to the Will of God, then ſhe diſpoſes of an Hour very innocently, tho' her *Mother* or her *Aunt* were not with her. But if the contrary to all this be true, if moſt of what ſhe there hears and ſees, be as *contrary* to the Piety and Purity of Chriſtianity, as *Feaſting* is contrary to *Faſting* ; if the Houſe which ſhe ſupports by her Money, and encourages by her Preſence, be a notorious Means of Corruption, viſibly carrying on the Cauſe of Vice and Debauchery, ſhe muſt not then think her ſelf ex-cus'd for being with her *Mother*.

Thirdly, THE ſame Perſon would perhaps think it ſtrange to hear one of her virtuous Acquaintance, giving the like Excuſe for going now and then to a *Maſquerade*.

Now

No w this Diverſion is new in our Country, and therefore People judge of it in the Manner that they ſhould, becauſe they are not blinded by *Uſe and Cuſtom* ; but let any one give but the true Reaſons why a Perſon of Virtue and Piety ſhould not give into ſuch Entertainments, and the ſame Reaſons will ſhew, that a Perſon of ſtrict Piety, ſhould keep at as great a Diſtance from the P*lay-houſe*. For the Entertainment of the *Stage* is as directly oppoſite to the P*urity* of Religion, and is as much the *natural Means* of Corruption, and ſerves all bad Ends in as high a Manner as *Maſquerades*, they only differ, as bad Things of the ſame kind may differ from one another. So that if the evil Uſe, the ill Conſequences of *Maſquerades*; be a ſufficient Reaſon to deter People of Piety, from partaking of them, the ſame evil Uſe and ill Conſequences of the *Stage*, ought to keep all People of Virtue from it. If People will conſult their *Temper* only, they may take the Entertainment of one, and condemn the other, as following the ſame Guide, they may abhor *Intemperance*, and indulge *Malice*; but if they will conſult Religion, and make that the Ground of their Opinions, they would find as ſtrong Reaſons for a conſtant Abhorrence of the *Stage*, as of *Maſquerades*.

FARTHER, She that is for going only to the *Play-houſe* now and then, with this Care and Diſcretion, does not ſeem to have enough conſider'd the Matter, or to act by Reaſon ; for if the *Stage* be an innocent and proper Entertainment, if in its own Nature it be as harmleſs and uſeful, as *Walking*, *Riding*, *Taking the Air*, or *Converſing* with virtuous People, if this be the Nature of it, then there is no Need of this Care and Abſtinence, a virtuous

Lady

Lady need not excuse herself, that she goes but very seldom. But if it be the very Reverse of all this, if it be that Fountain of Corruption and Debauchery, which has been observ'd, then to go to it at any Time admits of no Excuse, but is as absurd, as contrary to Reason and Religion, as to do any other ill Thing with the same Care and Discretion. If you should hear a Person excusing her Use of *Paint* in this Manner, that truly she painted but *very seldom*, that she always said her Prayers first, that she never us'd it on *Sundays*, or the Week before the *Communion*, would you not pity such a *Mixture* of Religion and Weakness? Would you not desire her to use her Reason, and either allow *painting* to be an innocent Ornament, suitable to the *Sobriety* and *Humility* of a Christian, or else to think it as unlawful at one Time as at another? Would you not think it strange that she should condemn *painting* as odious and sinful, and yet think, that the Regularity of her Life, the Exactness of her Devotions, and her Observance of Religion, might make it lawful for her to *paint now and then?* I don't doubt, but you plainly see the Weakness and Folly of such a Pretence for *painting* under such Rules at certain Times. And if you would but as impartially consider your Pretences for going sometimes to the *Play-house*, you would certainly find them equally Weak and Unreasonable. For *Painting* may with more Reason be reckon'd an *innocent Ornament*, than the *Play-house* an innocent Diversion; and it supposes a greater Vanity of Mind, a more perverted Judgment, and a deeper Corruption of Heart, to seek the Diversion of the *Stage*, than to take the Pleasure of a *borrow'd Colour*.

I

I know you are offended at this *Comparison*, because you judge by your *Temper* and *Prejudices*, and don't consider the Things, as they are in themselves, by the pure Light of Reason and Religion. *Painting* has not been the Way of your *Family*, it is supposed to be the Practice but of *very few*, and those who use it, endeavour to *conceal* it, this makes you readily condemn it; on the contrary, your *Mother* and your *Aunt* carry you to a *Play*, you see *virtuous* People there, and the same Persons that fill our *Churches*, so that your *Temper* is as much engag'd to think it lawful to go sometimes to a *Play*, as it is engag'd to think the Use of *Paint* odious and sinful. Lay aside therefore these Prejudices for a while, fancy that you had been train'd up in some Corner of the World, in the Principles of Christianity, and had never heard either of the *Play-house* or *P*ainting. Imagine now that you was to examine the Lawfulness of them by the Doctrines of Scripture. You would first desire to be told the Nature of these Things, and what they meant. They would tell you that *painting* was the borrowing of *Colours* from Art, to make the Face look more beautiful. Now tho' you found no express Text of Scripture against *painting*, you would find, that it was expresly against *Tempers* requir'd in Scripture; you would therefore condemn it, as proceeding from a *Vanity* of Mind, a *Fondness* of Beauty ; you would see that the Harm of *painting* consisted in this, that it proceeded from a *Temper* of Mind, contrary to the *Sobriety* and *Humility* of a Christian, which indeed is Harm enough, because this *Humility* and *Sobriety* of Mind is as *essential* to Religion, as Charity and Devotion. So that in judging according to Scripture, you would hold it as unreasonable to

paint

paint sometimes, as to be sometimes *malicious, indevout, proud,* or *false.*

You are now to consider the *Stage,* you are to keep close to Scripture, and fancy that you yet know nothing of P*lays.* You ask therefore first what the *Stage* or P*lay-house* is. You are told that it is a P*lace* where all Sorts of People meet to be entertained with *Discourses, Actions,* and *Representations;* which are recommended to the Heart, by beautiful Scenes; the Splendor of Lights, and the Harmony of Musick. You are told, that these Discourses are the Inventions of Men of Wit and Imagination, which describe imaginary *Intrigues* and *Scenes of Love,* and introduce *Men* and *Women* discoursing, raving, and acting in all the wild, indecent Transports of *Lust* and P*assion.* You are told that the Diversion partly consists of *lewd* and *prophane* Songs, sung to fine Musick, and partly of extravagant Dialogues between *immodest* Persons, talking in a Stile of *Love* and *Madness,* that is no where else to be found, and entertaining the *Christian Audience,* with all the the Violence of Passion, Corruption of Heart, Wantonness of Mind, Immodesty of Thought, and prophane Jests, that the Wit of the P*oet* is able to invent. You are told, that the P*layers,* Men and Women, are trained up to act and represent all the Descriptions of Lust and Passion in the *liveliest Manner,* to add a Lewdness of Action to lewd Speeches ; that they get their Livelihood, by *Cursing, Swearing,* and *Ranting,* for three Hours together to an Assembly of *Christians.*

Now though you find no particular Text of Scripture condemning the *Stage,* or *Tragedy,* or *Comedy,* in express Words, yet, what is much more, you find that such Entertainments are a gross Contradiction

tradiction to the *whole Nature* of Religion. They are not contrary to this or that particular Temper, but are contrary to that *whole Turn* of Heart and Mind which Religion requires. *Painting* is contrary to *Humility*, and therefore is always to be avoided as sinful. But the Entertainment of the *Stage*, as it consists of *blasphemous* Expressions, *wicked* Speeches, *Swearing*, *Cursing*, and *Prophaning* the Name of God, as it abounds with *impious* Rant, *filthy* Jests, *distracted* Passions, gross Descriptions of *Lust*, and *wanton Songs*, is a *Contradiction to every Doctrine* that our Saviour and his Apostles have taught us. So that to abhor *Painting* at all Times, because it supposes a Vanity of Mind, and is contrary to Humility, and yet think there is a lawful Time to go to the *Play-house*, is as contrary to common Sense, as if a Man should hold that it was lawful sometimes to offend against *all the Doctrines* of Religion, and yet always unlawful to offend against *any one* Doctrine of Religion.

IF therefore you was to come (as I supposed) from some Corner of the World, where you had been used to live and judge by the Rules of Religion, and upon your Arrival here, had been told what *Painting* and the *Stage* was; as you would not expect to see Persons of *religious Humility* carrying their Daughters to *Paint-shops*, or inviting their *pious Friends* to go along with them, so much less would you expect to hear, that *devout, pious* and *modest* Women carried their Daughters, and invited their virtuous Friends to meet them at the *Play*. Least of all could you imagine, that there were any People *too pious* and *devout* to indulge the Vanity of *Painting*; and yet not devout or pious enough to *abhor*

D   the

the Immodesty, Prophaness, Ribbaldry, Immorality, and Blasphemy of the *Stage*.

To proceed. A *polite Writer* (a) of a late Paper thought he had sufficiently ridiculed a certain Lady's Pretension to *Piety*, when speaking of her *Closet*, he says,

> *Together by her Prayer book and Paint,*
> *At once t' improve the Sinner and the Saint.*

Now whence comes it that this *Writer* judges so rightly, and speaks the Truth so plainly in the Matter of *Painting?* Whence comes it that the Generality of his Readers think his Observation just, and join with him in it? It is because *Painting* is not yet an *acknowledged Practice*, but is for the most Part reckoned a *shameful Instance* of Vanity. Now as we are not prejudiced in Favour of this Practice, and have no Excuses to make for our *own Share* in it, so we judge of it impartially, and immediately perceive its Contrariety to a religious Temper and State of Mind. This *Writer* saw this in so strong a Light, that he does not scruple to suppose, that *Paint* is as natural and proper a Means to improve the *Sinner*, as the Prayer-book is to improve the *Saint*.

I should therefore hope, that it need not be imputed to any *Sowreness* of Temper, religious *Weakness* or *Dulness* of Spirits, if a *Clergyman* should imagine, that the Prophaness, Debauchery, Lewdness, and Blasphemy of the *Stage*, is as natural a Means to improve the *Sinner*, as a *Bottle of Paint*; or if he should venture to shew, that the *Church* and the *Play-house* are as ridiculous a Contradiction, and

do

do no more suit with the *same* Person, than the *Prayer-book* and *Paint*.

Again, SUPPOSE you were told that the *holy Angels* delight in the Repentance and Devotion of Christians, that they attend at God's *Altar*, and rejoice in the Prayers and Praises, which are there offer'd unto God; I imagine you could easily believe it. you could think it very agreeable to the Nature of such good Beings, to see *fallen Spirits* returning unto God. Suppose you were told also, that these same heavenly Beings delighted to be with Men in their *Drunkenness, Revellings,* and *Debaucheries,* and were as much pleased with their Vices and Corruptions, as with their Devotions, you would know, that both these Accounts could not possibly be true; you could no more doubt in your Mind, whether *good Angels,* that delight in the Conversion and Devotion of Christians, do also delight in their Vices and Follies, than you can doubt, whether the same Person can be *alive* and *dead* at the same Time. You would be sure, that in Proportion as they delighted in the *Piety* and *Holiness* of Men, they must necessarily in the same Degree abhor and dislike their *Vices* and *Corruptions.* So that, supposing the Matter of our *Church-Service,* the Excellency of its Devotions, its heavenly Petitions, its lofty Hymns, its solemn Praises of the most High God, be such a glorious Service as invites and procures the Attendance of that *blessed Quire;* if this be true, I suppose you are as certain as you can be of the plainest Truth, that the *Filthiness,* the *Rant, Ribbaldry, Prophaness,* and *Impiety* of the *Stage,* must be the Hatred and Aversion of those *good Spirits.* You are sure, that it is as impossible for them to behold the *Stage*

D 2

with

with Pleasure, as to look upon the *Holy Altar* with Abhorrence.

CONSIDER a while on this Matter, and think how it can be lawful for you to go to a *Place*, where if a *good Angel* was to look with Pleasure, it would cease to be good? For as that which makes Angels good, is the same *right Temper* which makes you good, so the same Tempers which would render Angels evil, must also render you evil. You may perhaps tell me, that you are not an *Angel*. I grant it, neither are you Jesus Christ, neither are you God, yet you are called to be *Holy* as Jesus Christ was *Holy*, and *to be Perfect as your Father which is in Heaven is Perfect*. Though you are not an *Angel*, yet it is Part of your glorious Hope, that you shall be *as the Angels of God* ; so that as you are capable of their Happiness, you must think your self obliged to be as like them in your Temper, as the Infirmity of your present State will permit. If *Angels* are to rejoice in singing the Praises of God, though their Joy may exceed yours, yet you are as much obliged to your Degree of Joy in this Duty, as they are. Angels by the Light and Strength of their Nature, may abhor all Manner of Sin with stronger Aversion, a higher Degree of Abhorrence, yet you are as much obliged to abhor all Manner of Sin, as they are. So that it is no more lawful for you to delight in impure, prophane Diversions, which *good Angels* abhor, than it is lawful for you to hate those *Praises* and *Adorations* which are their Delight.

YOU are to consider also, that these *contradictory Tempers* are no more possible in the *same Men*, than in the *same Angels* ; 'tis no more possible for your Heart truly to delight in the Service of the Church, to be in Earnest in all its Devotions, and at the same

Time

delight in the Entertainment of the *Stage*, than it is possible for an *Angel* to delight in them both.

You may fansy that you relish these Entertainments, and at the same Time relish and delight in the Service of God, and are very hearty in your Devotions; you may fansy this, as *cruel* Men may fansy themselves to be *merciful*, the *covetous* and *proud* may fansy themselves to be *humble* and *heavenly-minded*; but then take Notice, that it is all but mere Fancy: For it is as impossible to be really devout with your Reason and Understanding, and at the same delight in the Entertainment of the *Stage*, as 'tis impossible to be really *charitable*, and delighting in *Malice* at the same Time. There is indeed a *Falseness* in our Hearts, a *Mechanism* in our Constitution, which will deceive those, who do not constantly *suspect* themselves. There are *Forms of Devotion*, little Rules of Religion, which are fixed in us by *Education*, which we can no more part with, than we can part with any other Customs, which we have long used. Now this makes many People think themselves mighty pious, because they find it is not in their Nature to forbear or neglect such and such *Forms of Piety*; they fansy that Religion must have its Seat in their Heart, because their Heart is so unalterable in *certain Rules* of Religion. Thus a Person is exact in his Times of Prayer, will perhaps think himself much injured, if you was to tell him that it is his *Want of Piety*, that makes him relish the Diversion of the *Stage*: His Heart immediately justifies him against such an Accusation, and tells him how constant he is in his Devotions; whereas it is very possible, that he may have but little more Piety, than what consists in some *Rules* and *Forms*, and that his Constancy to such Rules, may be owing

ing to the same Cause, which makes others constantly *sleepy* at such an Hour, that is, the mere *Mecha-*
nism of his Constitution, and the Force of *Custom*.
This is the State of Numbers of People, otherwise it
would not be so common, to see the same People constant and unalterable in *some Rules* of Religion, and
as constant and unalterable in *Pride*, *Passion*, and
Vanity.

Again, T H E R E are many other Instances of a
false Piety : Some People feel themselves capable of
religious Fervours, they have their Passions frequently
affected with *religious Subjects*, who from thence
imagine, that their Hearts is in a true State of Religion. But such a Conclusion is very deceitful.
For the mere *Mechanism* and natural Temper of our
Bodies, and our present Condition, may be the chief
Foundation of all this. Thus a *Lady* may find herself, as she thinks, *warm* in her Devotions, and
praise God at *Church* with a Sense of Joy ; she thinks
she is very good, because she finds herself thus *af-*
fected and *pleased* with the Service of the *Church* ;
whereas it may be, the very Reason why she is more
than ordinarily devout, and thinks it a Pleasure to
praise God, is, because she is going to a *Ball*, or a
Play, as soon as Divine Service is over. This agreeable Expectation has so put her Spirits in Order, that
she can be very *thankful* to God all the Time she
is at *Church*.

A N O T H E R has been pleased with the Compliments paid to her Person, she finds herself very *fine-*
ly dress'd, she is full of Joy under *such Thoughts*, and
so can easily break out into *Fervours of Devotion*,
and rejoice in God at a Time, when she can rejoice
in *any Thing*. These frequent Starts of Devotion
makes her think herself to be far advanced in Piety,
and

and she does not perceive that the *Height* of her Devotion is owing to the Height of her Vanity. Let
her but be *less pleased* with herself, let her be *unre-
garded, undressed*, without such *pleasing Reflections*,
and she will find herself sunk into a strange *Dulness*
towards Devotion.

THE same Temper is very frequent in *common
Life*; you meet a Person who is very fond of you,
full of Affection, and pleased with every Thing you
say or do; you must not imagine that he has more
Friendship for you, than when he saw you last, and
hardly took any Notice of you: The Matter is only
this, the Man is in a *State of Joy* at something or
other, he is pleased with *himself*, and so is easily
pleased with you, stay but till this *Flow of Spirits*
is gone off, and he will shew you no more Affection
than he us'd to do. This is the Religion of *Numbers*
of People; they are devout by *Fits and Starts*, in
the same Manner as they are pleased by *Fits and
Starts*, and their Devotion at those very Times is no
more a Sign of true *Piety*, than the Civility and
Compliments of a Person *overjoyed*, are Signs of true
Friendship. But still these little Flashes of Devotion make People think themselves in a State of Religion.

TAKE another Instance of a false Piety of another
kind: *Junius* has been orthodox in his Faith, a
Lover of Churchmen, a Hater of Hereticks, these
several Years; he is the first that is sorry for a *dangerous Book* that is come out, he is amazed what
People would be at by such Writings, but thanks
God there is Learning enough in the World to
confute them; he reads all the Confutations of *A-
theists, Deists*, and *Hereticks*, there is only one sort
of Books, for which *Junius* has no Taste, and that
is

is, Books of *Devotion*. He freely owns that they are
not for his Taste, he does not *understand their Flights*.

I f another Person was to say so much, it would
be imputed to his Want of Piety; but because *Junius* is known to be an Enemy to Irreligion, because
he is constantly at Church, you suppose him to be
a pious Man, though he thus confesses that he wants
the *Spirit of Piety*. It is in the same Manner that
Junius deceives himself, his Heart permits him to
neglect Books of Devotion, because his Heart is
constantly shewing him his *Zeal* for Religion, and
Honour for the Church; this makes him no more
suspect himself to want any Degrees of Piety, than
he suspects himself to be a Favourer of *Heresy*. If
he never thinks any ill of himself, if he never suspects any Falseness in his own Heart, if he is prejudiced in favour of all his own Ways, it is because
he is prejudiced in favour of all *orthodox Men*.
Junius reads much Controversy, yet he does not take
it ill, that you pretend to inform him in Matters of
Controversy; on the contrary, he never reads Books
of Devotion, yet is angry if you pretend to correct
him in Matters of that kind. You may suppose
him mistaken in something that he is always study-
ing, and he will be thankful to you for setting him
right; but if you suppose him mistaken in Things
that he never applies himself to, if you suppose that
any Body knows what *Humility, Heavenly-minded-
ness, Devotion, Self-denial, Mortification, Repentance, Charity,* or the *Love* of God is, better than
he, you provoke his Temper, and he won't suffer
himself to be informed by you. *Great Numbers* of
People are like *Junius* in this Respect, they think
they are very religious by listening to Instruction upon *certain Points*, by reading *certain Books*, and being

ing ready to receive farther Light, who yet cannot bear to be instructed in Matters where they are most likely to be deceived, and where the Deceit is of the utmost Danger. They will be thankful for your telling them the particular Times in which the *Gospels* were writ, for explaining the Word *Euroclydon*, or *Anathema Maranatha*, they will be glad of such useful Instruction, but if you touch upon such Subjects as really concern them in a high Degree, such as try the *State* and *Way* of their Lives, these religious People, who are so fond of religious Truths, cannot bear to be thus instructed.

WHAT is the Reason that when we consult *Lawyers*, it is not to hear Harangues upon the *Law*, or its several *Courts* ; it is not to hear the Variety of Cases that concern other People, but it is to be instructed and assisted in our *own Case* ? Why do we thank them for dealing impartially with us, for searching and examining into the true State of our *Case*, and informing us of every Thing that concerns us? What is the Reason that we apply to *Physicians*, not to hear the Rise and Progress of *Physick*, or the History of Disputes amongst them, not to hear of other People's Distempers, but to tell them our own *particular State*, and learn the *Cure* of our own Distempers ? Why do we thank them for being *nicely exact* in searching us out, for examining into every Part of our Lives, our Ways of *eating*, *drinking*, and *sleeping*, and not suffering us to deceive our selves with wrong Opinions and Practices ? What is the Reason why we act thus consistently, and in the same Manner, in both these Instances ? Now the only Reason is this, because in both these Instances we are *really in earnest*. When you are in earnest in your Religion, you will act as consistently

E   and

and in the same Manner there. When you desire *solid Piety*, as you desire *sound Health*, your chief Concern will be about your *own Disorders*; you will thank *Divines* and *Casuists* for making you their chief Care, you will be glad to have them examine and search into your Ways of Life, to be rightly informed of the Follies, Vanities, and Dangers, of your State. You will be glad to read those Books, and consult those *Casuists*, which are most *exact* and *faithful* in discovering your Faults, who question and examine all your Ways, who discover to you your *secret* Corruptions, and *unsuspected* Follies, and who are best able to give you the surest Rules of arriving at Christian Perfection; when you are in earnest in your Religion, you will as certainly act in this Manner, as you act in the same Manner with the *Lawyer* or *Physician*. Take this also for an undeniable Truth, that till you do act in this Manner, you are not in earnest in your Religion. This therefore is a good Rule to examine your self by. Do you find that you act in Religion as you do in other Cases, where you are in earnest? Are you as suspicious of your self, as fearful of Mistake, as watchful of Danger, as glad of Assistance, as desirous of Success, as in other Matters where your Life or Fortune are at stake, or where your Heart is engaged? Never imagine that your Religion is founded in a true Fear of God, and a hearty Desire of Salvation, till you find your self acting as you do in other Matters, where your Fears are great, and your Desires hearty. If you had rather read Books that *entertain* the Mind, than *correct* the Heart, if you had rather hear a *Casuist* examine other People's Lives, than your's, if you had rather hear him talk of the Excellency and Wisdom of

Re-

Religion, than be exact in trying the Excellency and Wisdom of your Way of Life, you must take it for granted, that you are not in earnest in the Reformation of your Life, and that there are *some Tempers* in you more strong, and powerful, that more rule and govern you, than the Fear of God, and a Desire of Salvation. To return now to my Subject

I H A D observed that People who are religious upon a true Principle, who are devout with their *Reason* and *Understanding*, cannot possibly either *relish* or *allow* the Entertainment of the *Stage*. I observed that these contradictory Tempers, a Delight in the Offices and Divine Services of the *Church*, and a Delight in the Entertainments of the *Stage*, are no more possible to be in the same *good Men*, than in the same *good Angels*. This made it necessary for me to step a little aside from my Subject, to consider some *false Appearances* of Religion, which are chiefly founded in *natural Temper*, *Custom*, *Education*, and the *Way* of the World; which yet so far deceive People, as to make them fancy themselves in a good State of Religion, while they live and act by another Spirit and Temper.

N o w I readily own, a Man may come up to these Appearances of Religion, he may carry on a Course of such Piety as this, and yet *relish* the Diversion of the *Stage*. It is no Contradiction for a Man to like to say his Prayers, to be often delighted with the Service of the *Church*, to hear *Sermons*, to read *Divinity*, to detest *Hereticks*, and yet find a constant *Pleasure* in the vain Entertainments of the *Stage*. The World abounds with Instances of People who *swear*, *drink* and *debauch*, with all these *Appearances* of Religion. Now as we are sure that where we

see

see these Vices, those Persons have only an *Appearance* of Religion, which is founded in something else than a true Fear of God; so wherever we see sober and regular People, Lovers of the Church, and Friends to Religion, taking the Pleasure of the *Stage*, we may be as sure that their Religion is *defective*, and founded in something that is *weak*, and *false*, and *blind*, that permits them to act so inconsistently. For the reasoning is full as strong in one Case as in the other. Now although I would not have People to be solely guided by what they feel, or think they feel in their own Minds, yet this we may depend upon, as certain in our Tempers, that we never *love* or *affect* any thing *truly*, but we *hate* and *avoid* all that is *contrary* to it in an equal Degree. So that we may be assured, that all that Love, or Zeal, or Affection, that we pretend for any thing, is but mere Pretence, and a *blind Motion*, unless it appears by a zealous lively Abhorrence of every thing that is *contrary* to it. Upon this Ground I again affirm, that it is impossible for truly religious People to *bear* the Entertainments of the *Stage*. For consider only the Matter in this short View. A truly religious Person is to love and fear, and adore God, with *all his Heart, and with all his Soul, and with all his Strength*; now I ask you, who it is that has this true Love of God? Is it he that delights in Prophaness at *all Times*? Or is it he that can bear with Prophaness *sometimes*? Or is it he that abhors and avoids it at *all Times* and in *all Places*? Which of these three hath a Right to be esteemed a true Lover of God? Now he that goes to a *Play* at any Time, though he may say that he does not delight in *Prophaness*, yet he must own that he can sometimes, and in some Places,

bear

bear with Prophaness. For Prophaness of some kind or other, is in most of our *Plays*, almost as common, as the Name of God in Scripture. But I will suppose it were only now and then, and that no Prophaness either of Thought or Expression happened above *twice* or *thrice* in an Entertainment, yet this is *Prophaness*, and he that can bear with *so much*, that can seek the Entertainment as a Pleasure, must acknowledge, that though he does not delight in Prophaness as such, yet he can *bear* with Prophaness for the Sake of *other Delights*. Now ask your self, has not he a truer Love of God whose Piety will not suffer him to bear with Prophaness at any Time, or in any Place, or for any Pleasure? Am I not therefore supported by plain Reason and common Sense when I affirm, that it is for Want of true Piety, that any People are able to bear the Entertainment of the *Stage*.

You see also that no higher Degree of Piety, is required to fill one with a constant Abhorrence of the *Stage*, than such a Piety, as implies an Abhorrence of Prophaness at *all* Times, and in *all* Places.

WHEN you are thus pious, when you thus love God, you will have a Piety, a Love of God that will not suffer you to be at an Entertainment that has any *Mixture* of Prophaness. Now as there must be this manifest Defect in true Piety, before you can bear with the Prophaness of the *Stage*; so if you consider every other Part of the Character of a truly religious Man, you will find, that there must be the same Defect run through the whole of it, before he can be fit for such Diversion.

You tell me that you love the *Church*, and rejoice at the Returns of Divine-Service, though you now and then go to a *Play*. Now consider what it

is

is which these Words mean, *If you love and delight in the Service of the Church,* then you love to be in a *State* of Devotion, you love to *draw near* to God, you love to be made sensible of the *Misery, Guilt,* and *Weight* of Sin, you love to *abhor* and *deplore* your Iniquities, and to lament the *Misery* and *Vanity* of human Life; you love to hear the Instructions of *Divine Wisdom,* to *raise* your Soul unto God, and *sing* his Praises; you love to be on your Knees *praying* against all the *Vanities* and *Follies* of Life, and for all the *Gifts* and *Graces* of God's Holy Spirit.

Now all this is implied in the true Love of *Church-Service;* for unless you love it *for what it is,* and because you feel its Excellency, your Love is only a *blind, mechanical* Motion; but if you love it in Truth and Reality, if you are thus affected with it, because all its Parts so highly suit the Condition of human Nature, whilst you are thus disposed, you can no more relish the *wicked Spirit* and *foolish Temper* of Stage-Entertainments, than *sincere, dying* Penitents can delight in the *Guilt* of their Sins.

Never imagine therefore, that you are sincerely affected with the *Confessions* of the Church, or that you are truly *glad* for the Return of those Hours, which humble you in the Sight of God, never imagine that you truly feel the Misery and Weight of Sin, or sincerely lament the Corruption of your Nature, whilst you dare go to the Fountainhead of Corruption, the Place where Sin reigns, and exercises its highest Power.

Never imagine that you have the Spirit of Devotion, that your Heart is renewed with the Holy Ghost, that it truly rejoices in the Means of Grace,

and

and the Hope of Glory ; never imagine. that it is
your Joy and Delight to worſhip God in the Beauty
of Holineſs, to ſend up your Souls to him in Prayers
and Praiſes, ſo long as the Way of the *Stage*, its
impious Nonſenſe, *vile* Jeſts, *prophane* Paſſions, and
lewd Speeches, are not your utter Abhorrence. For
it is not more abſurd to believe, that a *corrupt*, Tree
may bring forth *good Fruit*, than to believe, that a
pious Mind, truly devoted to God, ſhould taſte and
reliſh the Entertainment of the *Stage*. For the *Taſte*
and *Reliſh* of the Mind is a more certain Sign of
the State and Nature of the Mind, than the Quality
of *Fruit* is a Sign of the State and Nature of *Trees*.

H A D the *impure Spirits*, which asked our Bleſſed
Saviour, to ſuffer them to enter into the *Herd of
Swine*, ſaid at the ſame time, that it was their only *Delight* and *Joy* to dwell in the Light and Splendor of God, no one could have believed them, any
more than he could believe Light and Darkneſs to
be the ſame Thing.

W H E N you have the Spirit of Chriſt, when you
are devoted to God, when Purity, Holineſs, and
Perfection is your real Care, when you deſire to live
in the Light of God's Holy Spirit, to act by his
Motions, to riſe from Grace to Grace, till you are
finiſhed in Glory, it will be as impoſſible for you,
whilſt you continue ſo diſpoſed, either to *ſeek* or
bear the Entertainment of the *Stage*, as it is impoſſible for *pure* and *holy Spirits* to ask to enter into a
Herd of Swine. If you want the Delight of ſo corrupt an Entertainment, ſo contrary to the *Spirit* and
Purity of Religion, you ought no more to believe
your ſelf, when you pretend to true *Piety* and *Devotion*, than you ought to have believed thoſe *impure
Spirits*, if they had pretended to have been *Angels
of*

of Light. For this is absolutely certain, and what you ought carefully to confider, that nothing ever gives us any Pleafure, but what is *fuitable* to the *State* and *Temper* of Mind that we are then in. So that if the *Corruption,* the *Immorality,* the *prophane* Spirit and *wanton* Temper of the *Stage-Entertain-ment* can give you any Pleafure, you are as fure that there is *fomething* like *all thefe Vices* in your Heart, as you can be of any Thing that relates to a human Mind.

Laftly, A s k your felf, when you think that you have a true Love for Divine-Service, whether he is not a truer Lover of it, whofe Soul is fo *fashioned* to it, fo *deeply affected* with it, that he can delight in nothing that is *contrary* to it ; who can bear with *no* Entertainment that is made up of *Speeches, Paffi-ons, Harangues,* and Songs fo *opposite* to the Wif-dom, the Difcourfes, Inftructions, and Hymns, of Divine-Service. This I believe, you cannot deny, and if this cannot be denied, then it muft be owned as a certain Truth, that he who can bear with the *Stage-Entertainment,* has this farther Defect, that he wants the *true Love* of Divine-Service.

A g a i n, It is Part of a truly religious Man, to *love* the Scripture, and *delight* in reading them ; you fay this is your Temper, though you go to *Plays.* I anfwer, that it is for want of a true Love and Delight in the Scriptures, that you are able to relifh *Plays.* You may perhaps fo love the Scrip-tures, that you may think it your Duty to read them ; and defire to underftand them. But when you once fo love the Scriptures, as to *love* to be *like* them, to defire that the Spirit and Temper of Scripture, may be the *one Spirit and Temper* of your Life ; When, for Inftance, you love this Doctrine,

Strive

Strive to enter in at the strait Gate. If thy right Eye offend thee, pluck it out and cast it from thee. When you are of the same Mind with this Scripture, *be sober, be vigilant, because your Adversary the Devil, as a roaring Lion, walketh about seeking whom he may devour* (a).

When you are intent upon this Truth, *For we must all appear before the Judgment-Seat of Christ; that every one may receive the Things done in his Body* (b). When this Text has taken Possession of your Heart, *Seeing then that all these Things must be dissolved, what Manner of Persons ought ye to be in all holy Conversation and Godliness* (c)?

When you resign up your whole Soul to this Exhortation, *Take my Yoke upon you, and learn of me for I am meek and lowly in Heart* (d). When your Heart can truly bear you witness to this Doctrine, that you *put on the whole Armour of Christ, that you may be able to stand, that you live by Faith* and *not by Sight, pressing after the Prize of your high Calling.* When you thus love and delight in the Scriptures, when you thus enter into its Spirit and Temper, when its Purity is your Purity, its Fears, and Hopes, and Joys, are your Fears, and Hopes, and Joys, you will find your self one of those, who constantly and at *all Times* abominate the Folly, Impertinence and Prophaneß of the *Stage.*

Let me desire you, when you are dress'd for a *Play,* to read over our Saviour's Divine Sermon on the *Mount* before you go; try whether your Soul is full of the Spirit that is there taught, examine whether you then feel in your Heart such a Love of

F

the

(a) 1 Pet. iii. 8. (b) 2 Cor. v. 10. (c) 2 Pet. iii. 11. (d) Matth. xi. 29.

the Scripture, as to love *those Conditions* of Blessed-
ness that are there described, *Blessed are the poor in
Spirit, blessed are they that Mourn, blessed are they
that Hunger and Thirst after Righteousness.* Do
you find your self in these Heights of *Holiness?* Is
your Soul reform'd, purify'd and exalted according
to *these Doctrines?* Or can you imagine, that you
are *conforming* your self to those Doctrines, that you
depart from none of them, when you are preparing
your self for a Pleasure, which is the proper Pleasure
of the most corrupt and debauched Minds? *Blessed are the pure in Heart for they shall see God.*
Can you think that you are rightly affected with this
Doctrine, that you are labouring after this Purity,
that you are preparing to see God, when you are
going to an Entertainment, to which they ought only to go, who have no Thoughts of seeing God,
nor any Desires after that Purity which prepares us
for it?

Lastly, ANOTHER Virtue essential to Christian
Holiness is *Chastity,* our Blessed Saviour has given us
the Measure of this Virtue in these Words. *But I
say unto you, That whosoever looketh on a Woman to
lust after her, hath committed Adultery with her already in his Heart.* We are sure therefore that this
Virtue is not preserv'd, unless we keep our selves
clear from all immodest Thoughts and impure Imaginations; we are sure also that the Guilt of these
is like the Guilt of Adultery. This is the Doctrine
of Christ. Look now into the *Play-house,* and think
whether any Thing can be imagin'd more contrary
to this Doctrine?

FOR, not to consider the monstrous Lewdness and
Immodesty of the *Stage,* take it in its *best State,*
when some admir'd *Tragedy* is upon it. Are the
extra-

extravagant Paffions or *diftracted Lovers*, the impure
Ravings of *inflam'd Heroes*, the tender Complaints,
the Joys and Torments of Love, and *grofs Defcriptions* of Luft, are the *indecent* Actions, the amorous
Tranfports, the *wanton Addrefs* of the Actors, which
make fo great a Part of the *moft fober and modeft*
Tragedies, are thefe Things an Entertainment con-
fiftent with this Chriftian Doctrine? You may
as well imagine, that Murder and Rapine are con-
fiftent with Charity and Meeknefs. I hope it will
not now be faid, that I have fpent too much Time
upon this Subject. For tho' thefe Things are
generally look'd upon as *little*, becaufe they are
called *Pleafures* and *Diverfions*, yet they may as
juftly be called *Vices* and *Debaucheries*; they affect
Religion, as *Lies* and *Falfhood* affect it, in the very
Heart and Effence, and render People as incapable
of true Piety, as any of the groffeft Indulgencies
of Senfuality and Intemperance. And perhaps it
may be true, that more People are kept Strangers to
the true Spirit of Religion, by what are called *Pleafures*, *Diverfions*, and *Amufements*, than by *confefs'd
Vices*, or the Cares and Bufinefs of Life. I have
now only one Thing to beg of the *Reader*, that he
would not think it a fufficient Anfwer to all this, to
fay in general, That it is a Doctrine too *ftrict* and
rigid, but that he would confider every Argument
as it is in itfelf, not whether it be ftrict and rigid,
but whether it be falfe Reafoning, or more ftrict and
rigid than the Doctrine of Scripture. If it prefcribes
a Purity and Holinefs, which is not according to the
Spirit and Temper of the Scriptures, let it be reject-
ed, not as too ftrict and rigid, but as a Species of
falfe Worfhip, as vain and ridiculous as *Idolatry*:
But

But if what is here afferted be highly conformable to the moft plain Doctrines of Scripture, the faying that it is too ftrict and rigid, is of no more Weight againft it, than if it was faid, that it was *too true*. It is not my Intention to trouble the World with any particular Notions of my own ; or to impofe any unneceffary Rules, or fanfy'd Degrees of Perfection upon any People. But in declaring againft the *Stage*, as I have done, I have no more follow'd any particular Spirit or private Temper, or any more exceeded the plain Doctrine of Scripture, than if I had declared againft *Drunkennefs* and *Debauchery*. Let a Man but be fo much a *Chriftian*, as not to think it too *high a Degree* of Perfection, or too *ftrict* and *rigid* to be in Earneft in thefe two Petitions, *Lead us not into Temptation, but deliver us from Evil*; and he has Chriftianity enough to perfuade him, that it is neither too high a Perfection, nor too *ftrict* and *rigid*, conftantly to declare againft, and always to avoid the Entertainment of the *Stage*.

F I N I S.

SOME FEW
HINTS,

In Defence of

Dramatical Entertainments.

HEREAS there has of late been a warm Debate, about the Lawfulness of the Stage ; it appears a little odd, that no better Champion can be had, against the useful and polite Entertainment, than one, whose Opinions in Ecclesiastical Affairs, are condemned in our *Confession of Faith*, and a declared Opposer of sound Reasoning and good Manners. His sowr dogmatick Essay, against Dramatic Performances, was reprinted and sold about here, to the no small Terror of that bulky Part of Mankind, who never think

A   for

for themselves, and believe every Thing they hear, tho' frequently dubious of what they plainly fee. This muſt apologize for the following Pages; for tho there is nothing of real Weight or Force, in what he has advanced, yet there is too much, that tends to diſtract and perplex the Minds of thoſe, who are not us'd to argument, to rob them of the Tranquillity of Innocence, and terrify their Souls, with the ſhocking Appearance of imaginary Guilt. Nor would the pernicious Miſchief end here, but ſuch bugbear Notions, if they were to prevail, would be apt to diſcourage the Uſe of Dramatic Actions, which in all Ages and Nations, have always been eſteem'd the moſt noble and improving Diverſions, that the Mind at its Hours of Leiſure and Recreation, could be entertained with.

Mr. *Law*'s Arguments againſt the Stage, loſe all their Strength, and the frightful Fabrick falls from its falſe Foundation at once, by his advancing (without offering to prove it) *That it is ſinful to go to a Play.* Whenever that is proved, he deſerves not the Name of Chriſtian, that endeavours not to diſſwade the World from it, as ſincerely as he can; but that all Plays in general are vicious, was never proved, nor ever will.

That there are ſome Plays that have a Tendency to Wickedneſs, are full of Repreſentations that are profane, and Expreſſions ſhocking to a modeſt and Chriſtian Audience, is not denied; but is Love and tender Sentiments towards the virtuous Fair (the ſweeteſt and beſt Cement of humane Society) to be reckon'd a Vice, becauſe mercenary vile Strumpets are Women? Or is the Regard and Veneration, that we in Duty ought to pay to a

good

good Clergyman (the moſt valuable of Characters) to be in the leaſt leſſen'd, tho' a looſe Fellow ſhould ſteal himſelf into Orders, and entertain his Pariſhioners with Buffoonry, prove a Drunkard, Whore-maſter, and hereticaſ Incendiary; this is no Reflection on the *Holy Order*, he is to be thrown out, as every virtuous Government ſhould do profane Plays.

But good ones we'll never part with, as long as the reveal'd Will, and our Reaſon give Light to the contrary. To fly in the Face of a Government, ever zealous in making good Laws againſt every Immorality, and call, what they countenance and protect, the *Devil's Houſe*, *his Ground*, *worſhipping of Images*, &c. without diſtinguiſhing, is intolerable Rudeneſs, and Hair-brain'd Stupidity, and deſerves no Anſwer, but what is ludicrous; which ſhall be dropt for the Sake of ſome of juſt and pious thinking, who from a real good Principle, are afraid of admitting the Repreſentation of the beſt Plays, for Fear that the worſt ſhould get in with them; but we have no Reaſon to be apprehenſive of this Evil, conſidering the general Abhorrence, the Gentlemen and Ladies, and Generality of the inferior Rank in this Place, have to all Manner of Lewdneſs and Irreligion, together with Mr. *Aſton*'s good Senſe and Cautiouſneſs, to diſoblige a City, that he loves, and deſigns the Place of his Reſidence.

When it is *ſinful to go to a Play, it is ſinful*, is all that the angry Man has ſaid; and ſo I take my Leave of him, Mr. *S. P.* having anſwered all his groundleſs Aſſertions to every ones Satisfaction: Wherefore it comes more properly in our View, in the Purſuit

of

of this small Essay, to point out to a great many not versed in Stage-controversy, the Lawfulness and the Usefulness of Dramatic Entertainments, admitting none to be acted any way derogatory to our Morals, Manners and sound Reason. To give a short Character of all the *English* Plays most in Vogue, and distinguish the good from the bad, shall be the Subject of a future Essay, after an impartial Examination.

As to the Lawfulness of Plays, there is not one Text in the Scripture that condemns them : To argue there were no such Things in the Time of our Saviour and his Apostles, would shew the grossest Ignorance. As our blessed Saviour was born in the Days of *Augustus*, 'tis known by all Historians, that the shutting up of the Temple of *Janus* in his Reign, universally opened those of the Play-houses. Theatrick Representations, in all the Provinces of the spacious *Roman* Empire, were the then common publick Entertainment, and such they continued many Reigns after.

Now if Dramatic Entertainments were unlawful, it might raise a little Wonder, why the Apostles, that went forth by a special Command of the Almighty, to convert all Nations, preaching Repentance and the Kingdom of Heaven, they that so exactly perform'd that great Commission, as to arraign Vice and Impiety, from the Higest to the Lowest, in all its several Branches; not only pronounced *Anathema*'s against the more crying Sins, but read Divinity-Lectures, even upon the Wardrobe and Dressing-box, correcting the very Indecencies of the Hair, the Apparel, and each uncomely Gesture, &c. That these Missionaries of Salvation should travel thro' so many Nations, and meet at every Turn,

Theatres

Theatres and Stage-players ftaring them in the Face, and not once reprimand them, is Matter of very ferious Reflection.

Had the Play-houfe been the *Seat of Infection*, the *Chair of Peftilence*, or the *Devil's own Ground*, 'tis rational to think, that thofe Divine Monitors that fet Bars to the Eye, Ear and Tongue, to every fmalleft Avenue that might admit the Tempter, would hardly have left the broad Gates to the Play-houfe fo open, without one Warning to the unwary Chriftian, in fo direct a Road to Perdition; fuch a Difcovery would have been rather the early Favour of our Evangelical Guardians, tharr the extorted Confeffion of the Devil our Infernal Enemy, by the Mouth of a poffeft Woman, two hundred Years after. That as the Tale tells, (and worthy of the learned Mr. *Collier*'s quoting) " A certain Woman " went to the Play-houfe, and brought the Devil " home with her; (*the Play-houfe was well rid of* " *him*) and when the unclean Spirit was preft in " the Exorcifm, (*ufed at* Rome *to this Day*) and " afked how he durft attack her? anfwered, I have " done nothing but what I can juftify, for I feiz'd " her on my own Ground: " There's Law for ye, and 'tis plain to them that believes the Father of Lies, that neither Meffrs. *Collier* or *Law* were the firft that called the Stage the Devil's Mannor.

But to return to our Subject with Gravity: Some would argue, that the Silence of the Scriptures in this Cafe may be owing to this, " That to forbid, " often puts People in mind of what they fhould " not do; and thus the Force of the Precept is loft " by naming the Crime." Tho' this be faid by a Sainted Father, there is no more Reafon to agree

with

with him in such a ridiculous Assertion, than with Father *Origen* in his unmanly Error : For an unbiass'd Thinker will easily believe, that there is no Crime too black to be mentioned in the Oracles of Truth, when the very Sin that brought down Fire on *Sodom* has been recorded there. And certain it is, that the loud and repeated Fulminations of Vengeance. from the Mouths of the Patriarchs, Prophets and Apostles, against the most horrid Iniquities and Abominations, do not very well prove Scriptural Silence in such Cases. It is too audacious in any Christian to argue, or in the least to insinuate, that a Gospel Precept can possibly be ensnaring, and the Divine Command against a Sin, a Temptation to draw us into it; and consequently in some Cases safer, and more holy Prudence, to leave the Sinner to grope out his Way to Salvation, than to give him Light to guide him thither. That will never do; nor will particular Passages of Scripture that justly forbid the Enormities of vicious Representations, have any Force against the good and lawful. So we are safe still.

Further, it shews how little the Dramatic Poetry lay under the Gospel Censure, When we consider that Text of St. *Paul*, *Evil Communications corrupt good Manners*, as the Expression first of the Comic Poet *Menander*, 290 Years before CHRIST's Incarnation, and afterwards of the Apostle. Here it may be asked, Whether St. *Paul*, the most learned of the Apostles, in delivering the Divine Oracles, would have incorporated the Sayings of a Heathen Poet (that possibly had been spoke a hundred times over on the publick Stage, by a hireling Player) into the Gospel of Truth, notwithstanding the Morality of
the

the Expreſſion it ſelf; had Stage-plays in themſelves, or even Comedies, juſtly lain under the Character of being criminal, or Foolery unbecoming the Gravity of Chriſtians.

Another Inſtance of the Apoſtle's Reſpect for Dramatic Poets is in *Acts* xvii. 28. *In him we live, move, and have our Being; as certain of your own Poets have ſaid, For we are alſo his Offspring.*

In his Epiſtle to *Titus*, Chap. i. 12. ſpeaking of the People of *Crete*, he ſays, in the Words of *Epimenides* the Poet, Χρῆτες αεὶ ψεῦσαι, κακὰ θηεία, γαςέρες ἀργαί. *One of themſelves, even a Prophet of their own, ſaid, The* Cretians *are always Liars, evil Beaſts, ſlow Bellies : This Witneſs is true,* &c.

Here the Apoſtle has not diſdained to quote a Heathen *Poet,* nay and honour him with the Title of *Prophet :* Now therefore, as the Spirit of GOD ſpoke by the Mouth of the inſpired Penmen of the Scripture, we may venture to boaſt it gives ſome Reputation to the *Poet,* and no ſmall Vindication of the Innocence and Uſefulneſs of the Profeſſion, that the Holy Spirit himſelf has ſpoke in the Words of a *Menander* and an *Epimenides.*

In the Decline of the *Roman* Empire, when Butcheries of Chriſtians, Bear-garden Shews, and ſuch barbarous Diverſions (inſtead of the virtuous *Drama*) filled the publick Theatres with what was ſhocking to Chriſtians; the pious Fathers had then ſufficient Reaſon to forbid the Profeſſors of our holy Religion to be preſent at the Exhibition of ſuch diabolical Entertainments.

As it is plain that Stage-entertainments are not condemned in Scripture, ſo there are no Statutes in our Civil Law that make them criminal; but on the contrary,

contrary, they have been protected and encouraged by the best of Princes, and the most modest and vertuous of our Quality and Gentry. It is own'd that there are some old *Scots* Acts, made by the zealous Supporters of the *Romish* Worship, against the playing some Satiric Interludes, wherein were represented the ridiculous Frauds and Impositions of a wicked Popish Clergy; but such Acts make for us, when we think how great a Hand the renowned *Lord Lyon* Sir *David Lindsay*, and the other Wits in the Dawn of the Reformation, had in shaking off the Fetters of the See of *Rome.* Sir *David's* excellent Comedies, that were acted on the Play-green between *Leith* and *Edinburgh*, are sufficient Testimonies of this Truth. The valuable Interludes I have seen and read; and, with Permission of the Gentleman who has the only Manuscript Copies of them, the World shall have them very soon in Print.

Next, we shall take a short View of the Usefulness of Theatrical Entertainments, confining the Essay only to Comedy, Tragedy being class'd among the first kind of Epic Poetry, and not so liable to Censure, its Sentiments being noble, and Characters of the highest Rank, design'd to move our Pity for Vertue in Distress, and a pleasing Satisfaction to see the Wicked punished as they merit.

But Comedy, against which the Hue and Cry is raised, is a Representation of humane Life in a lower Class of Conversation: We visit the Palace for Tragedy, and range the Town for Comedy, *viz.* for the Follies, the Vices, the Vanities and the Passions of Mankind, which we meet with every Day: And the Comedian may join with the Satirist:

Quic-

Quicquid agunt homines, votum, timor, ira, voluptas,
Gaudia, difcurfus, noftri eft farrago libelli.

To confine our felves into as narrow a Compafs as poffible, under thefe three Heads; *viz. Folly, Knavery* and *Love,* we may not improperly rank the whole Characters in Comedy.

The Fools may be divided into three Claffes; the *Cuddens,* the *Cullies* and *Fops :* The Cudden is a natural Fool; the Cully, one of Man's making; and the Fop, one of his own making : And of all the three, there are numberlefs Degrees of more and lefs grofs. For the firft of thefe Fools, the *Sir Martin Mar-all,* or the *Sir Arthur Addle, &c.* I hope the Audience is in no Danger of taking Taint from thefe Characters; but as they afford healthful Mirth, fo their Abfurdities may be of ufe to the Improvement of many of their own Clafs, where that Mixture of natural Folly is not fo predominant over their better Senfe.

For the fecond, the made Fools, the Cully; here is the leaft Danger of a Contagion that Way : For that Difeafe is rather cur'd than catch'd from the Stage. The *Country Efquire,* the *Prodigal,* or the *Bubble, &c.* either cozen'd by *Sharpers, Spungers, Gamefters* or *Bullies;* or jilted by *Jades,* or fnared into any ruinous Folly of this Kind : In expofing thefe Characters, the Stage does the Work of a *Philofophy-School.* It carries the whole Force of *Precept* and *Inftruction,* to warn unwary Youth from the Snares and Quick-fands of Debauchry; it points him out the feveral Harpies that devour him; and inftead of taking Taint from the Stage, the very Sight of the Plague-fpots not gives, but expells the Contagion.

B   For

For the third Fool, the *Fop*; this indeed of all
Fools is the moſt incorrigible. The *Cüdden* wants
no good Will to be wiſer; and would learn Wit,
were he capable of it. The *Cully* indeed is capable
to be taught, but ſeldom learns till he has too well
paid for his Learning, ſometimes at no leſs Price
than his Ruin, when he buys the Knowledge of find-
ing himſelf a Chowſe. But of all Fools the *Fop* is
the blindeſt : His Faults are his Perfections, while
he looks upon himſelf as one of the compleateſt Cour-
tiers and Gentlemen; and by that means very hard
to be cured of the Fondneſs he has for his own
tawdry Picture. However, in all Theatres, where
any Fop is Auditor, he'll never play the *Narciſſus*
there, to fall in Love with his own painted Face,
in a Sir *Courtly Nice* or Lord *Fopington*'s Looking-
glaſs. This we may poſitively ſay, He that brings
not the Fop to the Play-houſe, ſhall never carry it
from thence; but he that brings it there, may depart
without it : And in all the Stage *Fop-pictures*, the
Stage bids ſo fair for mending that Fool too, that
if the Goodwill fails, the Fault is not in the Mirror,
the Hand that holds it, or the Light it ſets at; but
in the perverſe and deprav'd Optics that cannot ſee
themſelves there.

As to the ſecond Claſs, the *Villain*, the *Uſerer*,
the *Miſer*, the *Cheat*, the *Pandar*, the *Bully*, the
Hypocrite, and all the reſt of their Brethren in Iniquity; there is ſo little Danger from all their Stage-
pictures, that there is no Fear of falling in Love with
them : On the contrary, nothing can give one a
greater Averſion to theſe ugly Vices, than expoſing
of them in their proper Colours. And therefore
we'll paſs to the lewd Love-diſtempers in **Comedy**,
and

and see what Morality the more dangerous Contagion and Malignity from these counterfeited Diseases may produce.

First then, to shew how very little Influence the Stage Characters and Representations of Whoredom and Debauchry carry to the Temptation of the Audience, or the Corruption of Manners, or to make Lewdness look lovely even to the very Practisers of it; let us consider, that he that loves Whoredom, loves the Harlot purely as the Harlot, the Sin when it comes singly *in puris naturalibus,* with as little a Train at the Heels of it as possible : For no Man loves the Levity and Fickleness of the Harlot, her false Oaths and Tears, the Profuseness of her Vanity, the Insults of her Pride, the Mercenariness of her Lust, her ugly Diseases, and revengeful Spite. Every Man, nay the greatest Libertine himself, would have a fix'd Mistris, (if such a Creature of that Kind could be found in the World) that would bring *Love for Love.* The Man that loves the Wanton, loves not the Traitress nor the Hypocrite. The Syrene may be lovely, and her Music pleasing; but we are not over fond of her Rocks and Quick sands.

The same Argument holds on the other Side : The *Dalilah* herself loves a Character of Honour and Fidelity in her Paramour, not the Looseness of the Rover and Libertine. A *Dormant* himself is no tempting Character for a young Lady to fall in Love with, tho' one of the finest of the Rover-kind in our Comedies. The veriest wanton of that Sex is as much for Monopoly as the other, and care not for half Hearts, a Gallant divided between a *Lovet,* a *Bellinda* and a *Heriot.*

Now, as the Lovers, I mean the vicious Characters of Love in our Comedies, are generally set forth with some of these fore-mentioned Corruptions, *viz.* Levity, Hypocrisy, Infidelity, Avarice, Diseases, Murders, Poverty, Disgrace, &c. We meet the Jilt, the Debauchee, the Rover, false Vows, Love for Money, Treason for Love, or some other accumulated Vice, more than the bare Wanton, in all of them. All these therefore are so far from seducing the unwary Auditor, those inviting Charmers off of the Stage, by what he sees presented upon it, that they much rather become the Objects of his Abhorrence, and the unwary Mistakes of others, as Beacons erected to keep him from sinking his Soul, Health, Estate and Reputation; as the wise and inspired Preacher has done in the Description of the alluring Adultress, *Prov.* Chap. vii.

Besides the strict Morality of a Comedy, there must be an Allowance for harmless and cordial Mirth; *a merry Heart does good like Medicine*: And there cannot be more entertaining Characters than these of the Jilt and Strumpet, by affording the most ample Matter in the Conduct of the Play to gain this agreeable Mirth, which is one of the great Ends of Comedy, and what chiefly attracts the Audience thither.

The Jilt, for Instance, with her Windings and Wheedles to draw in her *Cully*, and her Artifice to secure and manage him; the false Strumpet with her Fawnings and Flatteries to lull her Keeper's Jealousy, her Starts and Fears at every Alarm, her whole Arts to cover the Hypocrite, and her Surprise and Confusion at her Detection, (for Comedy does that Dramatic Justice, to bring her to Shame and other
ther

ther 'Punifhments) as they afford Plot, Défign and
Contrivance, *&c.* are the higheft Jeft in Comedy;
it is not the Lewdnefs of a vicious Character that
recommends it to the Audience, but the witty Turns,
Adventures and Surprifes in thofe Characters that
make them fo acceptable; for without this, the Play
droops and dies.

And to fhew this, when an ingenious Author,
(fuch as the late Secretary *Addifon,* Sir *Richard Steel,*
&c.) raifes the fame Mirth on the moft vertuous
Foundation; fuch Comedies fhall be as much Favou-
rites as the others; for Inftance, *The Drummer, Sir*
Solomon Single, Grief a la mode, and many other Comedies, where the Love is all honourable. In fine,
it is the Wit, and not the Vice of the Compofure
that gives Life to the Performance. A dull Reprefentation of Vice or Virtue fhall be equally hifs'd off
the Stage; and undoubtedly, the Satyric Expofure
of Debauchry, with all its Treacheries Wiles, Delufions, Impoftures, *&c.* has more of the Antidote
than the Poifon.

There's a vaft Difference betwixt liking the Picture and the Subftance; a Man may be very well
pleas'd with a Foreft work Piece of Tapeftry, with
the Lyons, Bears, Wolves, *&c.* but not fond of
their Company in Flefh and Blood; and confequent-
ly, (as we have obferv'd) a Jilt may give Diverfion
upon the Stage, and be our Averfion off it.

Nay further, we dare be fo bold to tell fome hear-
fay Cafuifts, who highly refent the picturing of a
Rake, endeavouring to (what they call) finifhing of
an Alderman, that we could find them Matter of
very good Inftruction, from a Character of this Kind
drawn by the ingenious Mr. *Congreve,* if the good
old

old Gentlemen would but now and then attend the Play-house. We doubt not but an *Isaac Fondle-wife*, in the *Old Batchelor*, would be a very seasonable Monitor to a reverend Dotard of Sixty three, to warn him against matching with the Vivacity of sixteen: Nor can I think it such a bad Part of the Dramatic Poet, but rather a true Poetic Justice, to expose the Unreasonableness of such superannuated Dotage, that can blindly think or hope, that Wealth, and a bare Chain of Gold has Magic enough in its Circle to bind the Fidelity of so unequal a Match, a Match so contrary to the holy Ordinance of Matrimony! a Folly at these Years that deserves the severest Lash.

One Thing mightily offends some Snarlers, *viz.* that our modern Plays make our Libertines of both Sexes Persons of Figure and Quality; a Fault never practis'd by the Ancients.

Now, this is so far from a Fault in Comedies, that there is a Necessity for these Characters, and a Virtue in such a Choice: For as the greatest Part of the Audience are Quality, and Persons of Distinction; if we would make our Comedies instructive in the exposing of Vice, we must not lash the Follies of Porters, to mend the Faults of a Court.

And as the instructive Design of the Play must look as well to the cautioning of Vertue from the ensnaring Conversation of Vice, as the lashing of Vice it self. Thus the Court Libertine must be a Person of Wit, Cunning and Politeness, and other Accomplishments of a fine Gentleman, (the Court Ladies receive no Visits from Ruffians.) Every Fool would fly from a Devil with a cloven Foot. That Devil then must have all the Appearance of Honour, that would seduce

duce Honour; and therefore it is those very Pictures the Stage must present: Tho' indeed we own it a Fault in an Author, to allow a polite Villain to be the Heroe of, and meet with no Disgrace or Punishment in his Play.

The *Plain-dealer* speaks well to this Purpose, and justifies this Choice of Characters for the *Drama*. " Who betrays, over-reaches or cheats you, but " your Friend? Your Enemy is not trusted with " your Affairs. Who violates the Honour of your " Wife, but your Friend? Your Enemy is not ad- " mitted into your Family."

Who therefore are those dangerous Friends of Quality, but their Bosom-conversation? and who are they, but their Equality? And therefore, for an instructive Draught for Comedy, who so proper to sit to her Pencil, as Quality?

Besides, Comedy opens a wrong Door to let in a Taint of Lust. Lust is the Product of Thought and Meditation, not the Child of Laughter. The Auditor must have a much more serious Face, than he wears at a light Comedy, to take so deep and fatal an Impression; unless that we could suppose, that the Jest of a Comedy should open his laughing Mouth so wide, as to let down a Lust like a Witch's Ball of Pins. Now, besides many equally diverting Objects in the same Landskip, the whole Stage is new furnished every Day, and a new Collection of Paintings for the next Entertainment. And if the Movement, Gesture or Equipage, have any such dangerous Force, here is not one Movement one Day, but what is quite altered the next; and so Change upon Change, *&c.* that in the infinite Variety of the Stage, here's no dwelling upon one darling Object, to run any
such

such Danger of Infection : For the whole Stage Mercury is too volatile to fix. But what *Quixote* Windmills cannot an Enthusiast raise, then battle the Giant of his own Creation!

But further, saith Mr. *Collier*, how can ye defend Duelling, and encouraging of Revenge, so contrary to the Gospel Precept of Forgiving ?

It is not to be defended, and is frequently ridicul'd, and the hectoring Bully brought upon his Marrow-bones, by Gentlemen of superior Worth and honourable Courage, who make the mistaken Fool a Present of his Life for his future Instruction.

We acknowledge our Saviour's Doctrine of Forgiveness is the highest Characteristic of Christianity, and a Perfection that comes nighest to the Great Original of Mercy that delivered it : But to examine what Consequence must follow the universal Stretch of a Divine Precept, please consider.

By these Divine Commands of our Saviour to the literal Extent, in the first Place, I must neither sue in Law or Equity for the Recovery of a just Right, or Reparation of any Wrong whatever : For the Prosecution of Law is directly opposite to this Forgiving Doctrine.

So here's the Courts of Judicature shut up immediately ; nay, if the Precept obliges me to the same Resignation of my Coat to the Thief that has robb'd me of my Cloak, I am so far from licensed to take that Christian Revenge, *viz.* the Prosecution of publick Justice upon him, that the very Judge, instead of arraigning the Robber or Felon at the Bar for the Breach of a Humane Law, should rather stand obliged to arraign the Prosecutor for breaking a Divine one. Here's the very Law it self arraigned, as
little

little less than Antichriftian, for punifhing that Inju-
ry which the good Gofpel Precept exprefly commands us to forgive even feventy Times feven. But
to reconcile the Gofpel with the moral Precept, it
is obvious to every thinking Chriftian, that it is the
penitent Offender, that makes a Retaliation, or fhews
a Willingnefs to do it if it were in his Power, and
asks Forgivenefs of the wrong'd, that can claim to
this God-like Humanity.

Nay, by this forgiving unrevenging Doctrine un-
warrantably pufh'd home; here's *Paffive Obedience*
and *Non-refiftance* fet up with a Vengeance, not only in Submiffion to terrible Tyranny, but even to e-
very diminitive arbitrary Thief and Ruffian to be
Lord and Mafter of my Purfe, Coat, Houfe, &c.
with a general Goal Delivery, Oppreffion, Theft,
Rapin and Villany let loofe, and the *Homo homini
lupus* at free Difcretion to fpoil, ravage and over-
run the whole World, while the meek refigning forgiving Chriftian is the tame bleeting Sheep before
him.

Further, I find one of the ill-natur'd Writers a-
gainft the Stage, after he has tautologiz'd himfelf
almoft out of Breath, exclaim as angrily at the *Vanity*, as at the greater Immoralities of the Stages,
and votes for their Exclufion even for that Offence
alone; but if he'll make a fair diftributive Juftice to
all proper Vanities, (for we will not allow corre-
ctive Reprefentations and moral Satyr to be of the
ufelefs or pernicious Lift) I am afraid he'll fet up a-
nother Doctrine that may prove hurtful to the Government, and very difobliging to Thoufands; for
if the Vanity-fhop, the Play-houfe, (as he calls it)
muft go down, pray let the Vanity-fhops, the *Em-
broiderer,*

C

broiderer, the Lace-man, the Feather-man, the Ribbon-weaver, the Confectionary, the Toy-shops and Tavern, cum multis aliis, come in for a Snack; for there is not one of all these, tho' not unlawful, yet are utterly useless to the real Wants of Life, and deal in more dangerous Vanities; for while the Stage only raises an innocent Tear or a Laugh, these other Vanities are very often the dangerous Nurses of Pride and Sensuality, more capital Faults.

Before I take Leave of this Subject, I must remark a Piece of unfair Dealing in Mr. Law, when he quotes the eminent Archbishop Tillotson condemning bad Plays. I found that he had prevaricated so vilely in it, that the Hypocrisy became immediately manifest; for, like the Devil quoting Scripture, he has omitted the former Part of the Passage, because it makes directly against him. It is as follows.

" To speak against Plays in general may be
" thought too severe, and that which the present
" Age cannot so well brook, and would not per-
" haps be so just and reasonable, because it is very
" possible they might be fram'd and govern'd by
" such Rules, as not only to be innocent and divert-
" ing, but instructive and useful, to put some Vices
" and Follies out of Countenance, which cannot
" perhaps be so decently reprov'd, nor so effectu-
" ally exposed and corrected any other Way."

Here the learned and worthy Bishop agrees in all that we have advanced: And many will allow his Authority to be good.

But what is all this to us, (say many of the lower Rank of Inhabitants,) we do not give our selves the Trouble about examining whether your Shows be lawful or no, we leave that to our Betters, and can
believe

believe as they bid us; but when Money is so scarce, are we to encourage People to pick it up from us, and carry it off.

My honest well-meaning Brethren, allow me to convince you of your Error, and shew you in few Words, that the Effect must be quite contrary.

For first you are to consider, that any Money the Players receive, it is from Persons of Quality, Gentlemen and Ladies, whose Fortunes can as easily spare forty or fifty Shillings in a Winter Season, as we can do Twopence; and what is it to us, if they amongst them have a mind to keep a Dozen Servants extraordinary, that can make two three Hours in an Evening agreeable to them; and they are such Gentlemany Servants, truly, as rarely put much of their Gains out to Usery, but have Difficulty enough to make both Ends meet. This can be nothing to our Loss, since they cannot live amongst us without the necessaries of Life. To demonstrate how little capable they are to harm us by carrying off our Money, we shall allow them to take in for their Tickets *L.* 60 *Sterling per* Month, which is at the Rate of *L.* 7 or 8 each Playing Night, a proper *medium* betwixt *L.* 10 or 11 their highest, and *L.* 4 or 5 their lowest. 'Tis own'd, when a Person of Distinction has a mind to make a Benefitnight, they may rise the Height of an *L.* 18 or 20 Night, but this is not frequent; but to my Calculation again, *L.* 15 *per* Week, eleven Persons, we must first substract at least *L.* 5 each Week for the needful Charges of the Theatre, (poor as it is at present) in Rent, Candle, printing Bills and Tickets, Wright-work, Servants of different Kinds, *&c.* not to mention Dues paid to the Master of the Revels

and

and some others; wherein Mr. *Aston* has acted honourably; who being Director, and one who can afford it, has laid out above *L.* 200 for fine Cloaths, and other Things proper for his Business, and has for this, as it is his due, more in the Dividend than the rest; what that is we are not to enquire into, but divide *L.* 10 a Week fairly amongst eleven People, and what they can carry off of that, after Eating, Drinking, Lodging, Supplies of Apparel, &c. I leave you to judge; but this Objection I remove all at once, by telling you that Mr. *Aston* is resolv'd to live and die in this Place.

Thus, as they can do us no harm by taking our Money, I argue next, that they are capable to do us much good; for none will deny, that the more genteel and pleasing Entertainments there are in a City, it will be the more engaging to Persons who can afford it, to leave their lonely Seats in the Winter Season, and reside with us: And for this Purpose we ought to endeavour all we can to make the Good Town agreeable to such who are the Support of it, without whom we might all leave out Peuter Vessel and Tea-kettles in the Lumber-houses to pay Stent and Annuity, and skip to the bent. This is so plain a Case, that I shall not insist upon it: But if the Question had been put to me, Whether Mr. *Aston* should be discharged acting within the Town, (as he had done with Applause the two former Sessions) or have a Play-house built for him at our Charge? I would have voted for the building; and believe me to be as sincere a Well-wisher to the Prosperity of *Edinburgh*, as any Citizen within its Walls.

We must remove another false Objection, founded upon the first Mistake of Plays being unlawful, That

Players

Players cannot be the beft of Men. But Plays are lawful, and Actors may be good Men: For Inftance, Mr. *Shakfpear* and *Betterton* were, and Mr. *Wilks* and Mr. *Mills* are good moral Men and Chriftians, who devoutly join in all the facred Inftitutions. Mr. *Afton* and his Family behave themfelves, to my certain Knowledge, with Sobriety, Juftice and Difcretion, pays his Debts without being dunn'd, is of a charitable Difpofition, avoids the intoxicating Bottle, and in every other Light appears what we call an honeft Moralift. For his Principles about the more refin'd Diftinctions of Religion, I'll not take upon me to condemn or juftify, he being of the Church of *England* Communion, a Religion different from mine, who am a Member of the prefent Eftablifhment of the Church of *Scotland*.

To conclude, it is at this Day evident, how great Advantage accrues to particular States by encouraging People of all Ranks and Employs to fettle among them, by indulging them with Candor, Freedom and Benevolence. Thus *Britain* was Gainer by encouraging ingenious Men, which *France* loft by perfecuting them out of their own Country. How by fuch Means is the late barbarous Empire of *Mufcovy* become formidable, and much more polite? Does not *Holland*, that once diminutive Republick, by fuch Policy fubfift, and advance in Riches and Prowefs fuperior to other Nations much larger in Extent? While *Spain* is half a Defart, and impoverifhed, by a tyrannous Inquifition, Bigotry, Superftition, Oppreffion, Perfecution and blind Ignorance, which implicitly hurry the Populace into overt Acts of unjuftifiable Dealing; by which they ruine their Country, and render themfelves odious to Men of Senfe and found Religion.　　　　　　　　**Now**

Now after all, my dear Fellow Citizens, pray take a short Review of the Opinions of the wisest and most potent Nations in their most flourishing State. Their Sentiments and Encouragement of Plays, for 2500 Years since, down to this present Day; the Reasonableness of such Entertainments, and the Advantages that our Good Town may receive by them; their instructive Use, their Innocence, and there being no Laws against them either Sacred or Civil; must surely in the whole (unless possest with singular and absurd Opinions) cause you acknowledge, that we ought to invite Mr. *Aston* to settle among us, and bring his Substance hither to deposite it in our Bank, (which he is resolved to do, if not driven from us by main Force) and protect and shelter him from all Injuries, and every rude Insult; ever remembring that amiable Picture of Charity that the Apostle has drawn, *This Bond of all Perfections is kind, not easily provoked,* &c.

Since it is generally allowed, by all who have read Tragedy and Comedy, and have seen them acted, that they are in themselves lawful, improving, and innocently diverting; we are not to have great Regard to such as violently condemn them, who at the same time will judiciously own, they never were so idle or wicked either to read or be present at the acting any one of them. Such must have a vast Opinion of Mr. *Collier* and Mr. *Law's* superior Judgment to the Legislature of the Nation: Which two Gentlemen, like losing Gamesters, only fell a railing after they had lost their Benefices for not complying with the Government.

Nor does it any more derogate from the Character of a Comedian to gain his Bread by his great

Pains

Pains he takes to pleaſe, than it does from others who think themſelves a Character far above him, yet would take it amiſs to be vilipended with the Name of *mercenary*. Of old indeed, when the *Grecian* and *Roman* Stages were in all their Glory, perhaps they took not in a ſmall Price of a few Tickets for ſupplying their Neceſſities; when the Tragic Poets were believed able to inſpire their Countrymen with the Love of Liberty, of Vertue, and of true Honour, and with a magnanimous Contempt of Death for the publick Good. This may be gathered from the unanimous Conſent of *Greece*, and particularly from the Honours done by the *Athenians* to their Dramatic Poets, who made them Governors of Provinces, Generals of their Armies, and Guardians of the publick Liberty: For when the *Athenians* ſettled a greater Fund for ſupporting the Magnificence of their Theatric Repreſentations, than for the Maintenance of their *Fleets* and *Armies*, we may juſtly conclude that it was their Opinion, that the Tragic Poets, by conſtantly ſetting forth before them the Calamities of Tyrants, defended them from far more dangerous Enemies than thoſe their Armies were ſent to encounter; and that was, from their own aſpiring Citizens. As no People were ever more jealous of their Liberties, than the *Athenians*; none ever knew better, that Corruption and Debauchry are inconſiſtent with Liberty: And therefore it never in the leaſt entred into the Thought of that great and wiſe People, that Corruption and Debauchry were the natural Effects of Dramatic Entertainments; for which the great *Ariſtotle* wrote Rules, and the divine *Socrates* aſſiſted *Euripides* in making his Tragedies.

That

That the *Romans* did not yield to the *Grecians*, in the Esteem they had for Dramatic Entertainments, and the Belief that they were capable of contributing to the Glory and Felicity of a mighty State, and the Honour of the Authors of them; we may gather from the Actions of their wisest Statesmen, their greatest Captains, and their severest Philosophers; who not only encouraged them, but vouchsafed to write them themselves. *Scipio* the wise and vertuous *Scipio*, wrote Comedy with that conquering Hand that won the Empire of the World at *Zama*. *Augustus Cæsar*, as famous for the Arts of Peace as his Success in War, renown'd for the wholesome Laws he enacted, and for his reforming the Manners of the People, begun the Tragedy of *Ajax*; tho' he could not finish it, but found it easier to make himself Emperor of the World, than a great Dramatic Poet. *Cicero*, the Champion of the *Roman* Liberties, in twenty Places of his Philosophic Treatises quotes the *Roman* Tragic Writers: And *Seneca*, who by so many admirable Lessons of moral Vertue has obliged all the Lovers of Wit and Goodness for ever, did not think Writing of Plays an Employment at all below him.